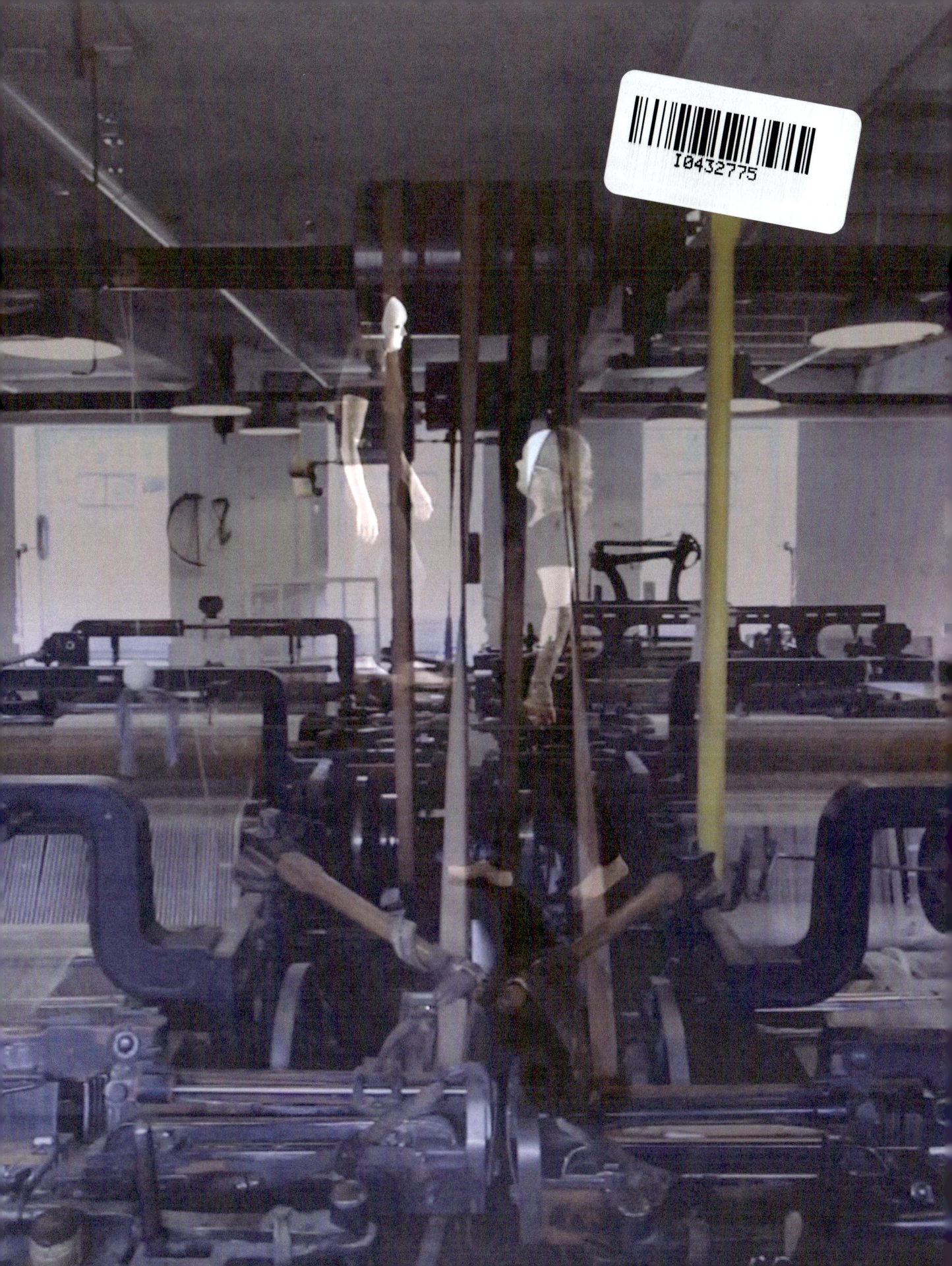

Cover image:

© Hannah Beatrice Photography 2019

Photography; copyright © Hannah Beatrice Photography 2019,

© Gareth Jones Photographer 2019.

Published by: Elizabeth Kwant Art 2020

Text © The Authors 2019

This book may not be reproduced in whole or in part in any form without written permission from the publisher.

www.elizabethkwant.com

AM I NOT A WOMAN AND A SISTER

by Elizabeth Kwant

A practice based research project co-creating a new artist's film in collaboration with female survivors of modern day slavery, in partnership with The International Slavery Museum and national charity City Hearts.

'every image of the past that is not recognised by the present as one of its own concerns, threatens to disappear irretrievably.'
Walter Benjamin

Acknowledgements

Elizabeth Kwant would especially like to thank; The women* (To protect their identity the women have not been named), Jean-François Manicom (Acting Curator, The International Slavery Museum), Beth Piner (Health & Wellbeing Coordinator, City Hearts), Steve Watson (North West Regional Manager, City Hearts), Magdalen Bartlett Luambia (Choreographer), Lucia Ceuvas & Fred Coker (Armadillo Productions), David Lascelles (8th Earl of Harewood), Diane Lascelles (Countess of Harewood), Nicola Stephenson (Exhibitions and Projects Producer, Harewood House Trust), Sarah Sarhandi (Musician, Composer), Mark Devereux Projects (Artist's Professional Development Mentoring), Sara Jaspan (Independent writer), Hannah Beatrice (Photographer), Clare Brown (Quarry Bank Mill).

'Am I not a woman and a sister' has been supported using public funding by the National Lottery through Arts Council England.

With special thanks to The International Slavery Museum & National Museums Liverpool, City Hearts, Mark Devereux Projects and Harewood House Trust.

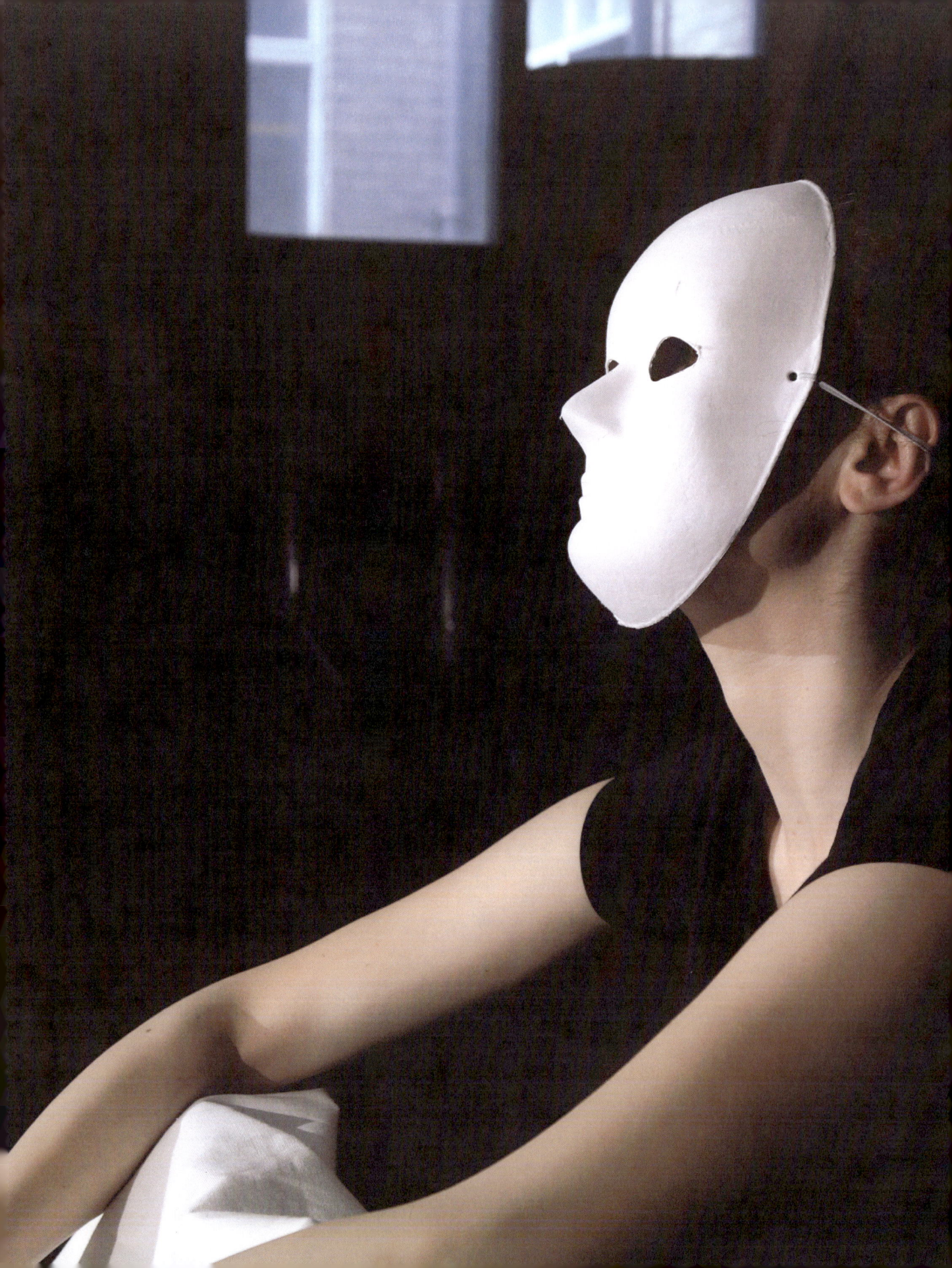

Contents

Acknowledgements — 5

Introduction — 9
by Jean-François Manicom

Am I not a woman and a sister — 15-28
by Sara Jaspan

Conversations with the women — 53-57

Biography — 58

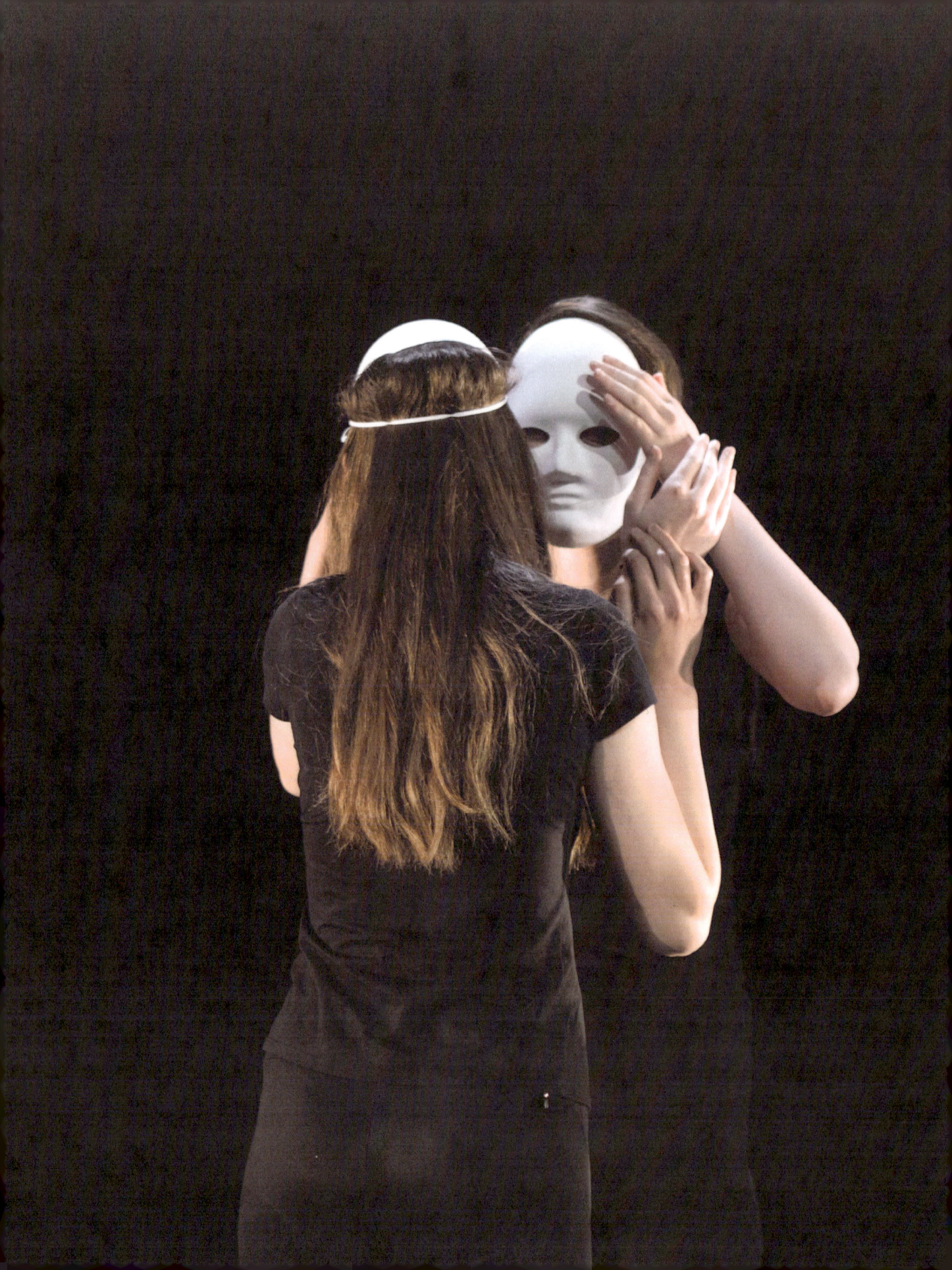

Introduction

by Jean-François Manicom

This is not quite a cotton thread with which their hands are playing: it is rather with their destiny, the fragile but surviving thread representing the life of millions of ancestors.

This is not quite a distaff that falls on the floor and bounces: it is rather the hope of generations of women, falling down but bouncing back centuries after centuries.

Those are not quite the Quarry Bank Mill machines we see and hear: it is rather the unstoppable and greedy industrial European machine adjusting to the plantation system.

This is not quite the library of Harewood House, those are not quite its gardens: rather, it is the repressed guilt, hidden within the secrets of wealth and in the unsaid apology.

This is not quite a dance it is rather bodies doing their best to move again and coming back to life.

This is not quite music it is rather sounds of muffled voices, calling for help and chanting for hope.

This is not quite a room with four screens it is rather the historical heart and geographical environment of a unique place in Europe.

It has not been quite a co-curation: rather, the work is made of multiple and subtle layers of knowledge, feelings, archives, expertise, pains, hopes, labour, skills, self-dedication, trust, in total hours of work that brought together agency and resilience.

It is not often that we can see ideas and emotions together in the same images. In *Am I not a woman and a sister* we can feel the depth of both, unfolding in the slow and hypnotic performance recorded on the screen.

At the International Slavery Museum, our constant mission is to help visitors understand how something as absurd as slavery took place, comprehend something incomprehensible. With elegance, modesty and gravity, Elizabeth Kwant established a relationship of trust and collaboration with women who suffered in their flesh. They are the Parcae who thread a new connection and embodied relationship. Their bodies become what links two traumatic histories: that of Transatlantic Slavery and that of modern slavery in its many versions.

This is not quite Contemporary Art: It is more than Art.

Jean-François Manicom is the acting curator for The International Slavery Museum.

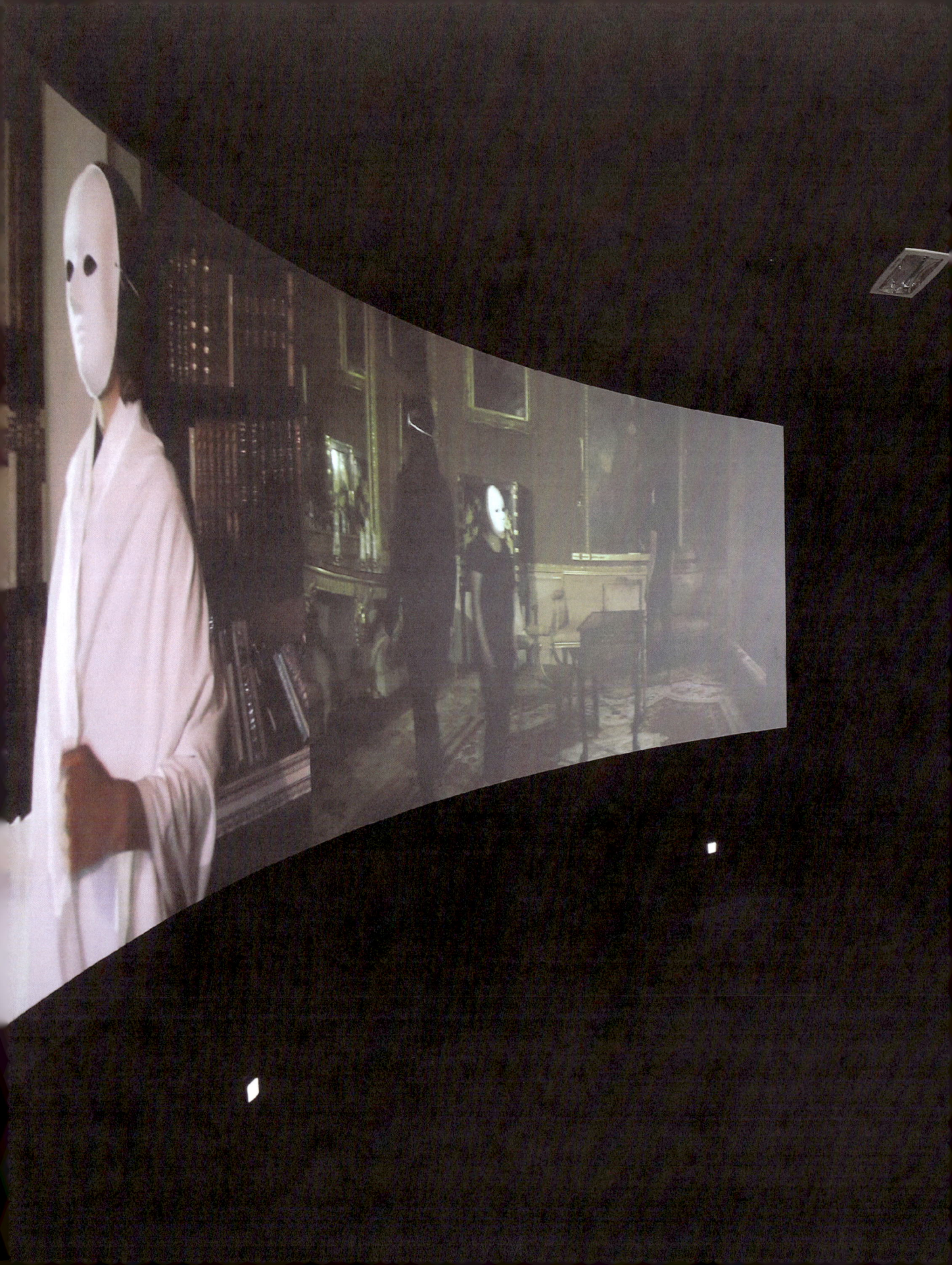

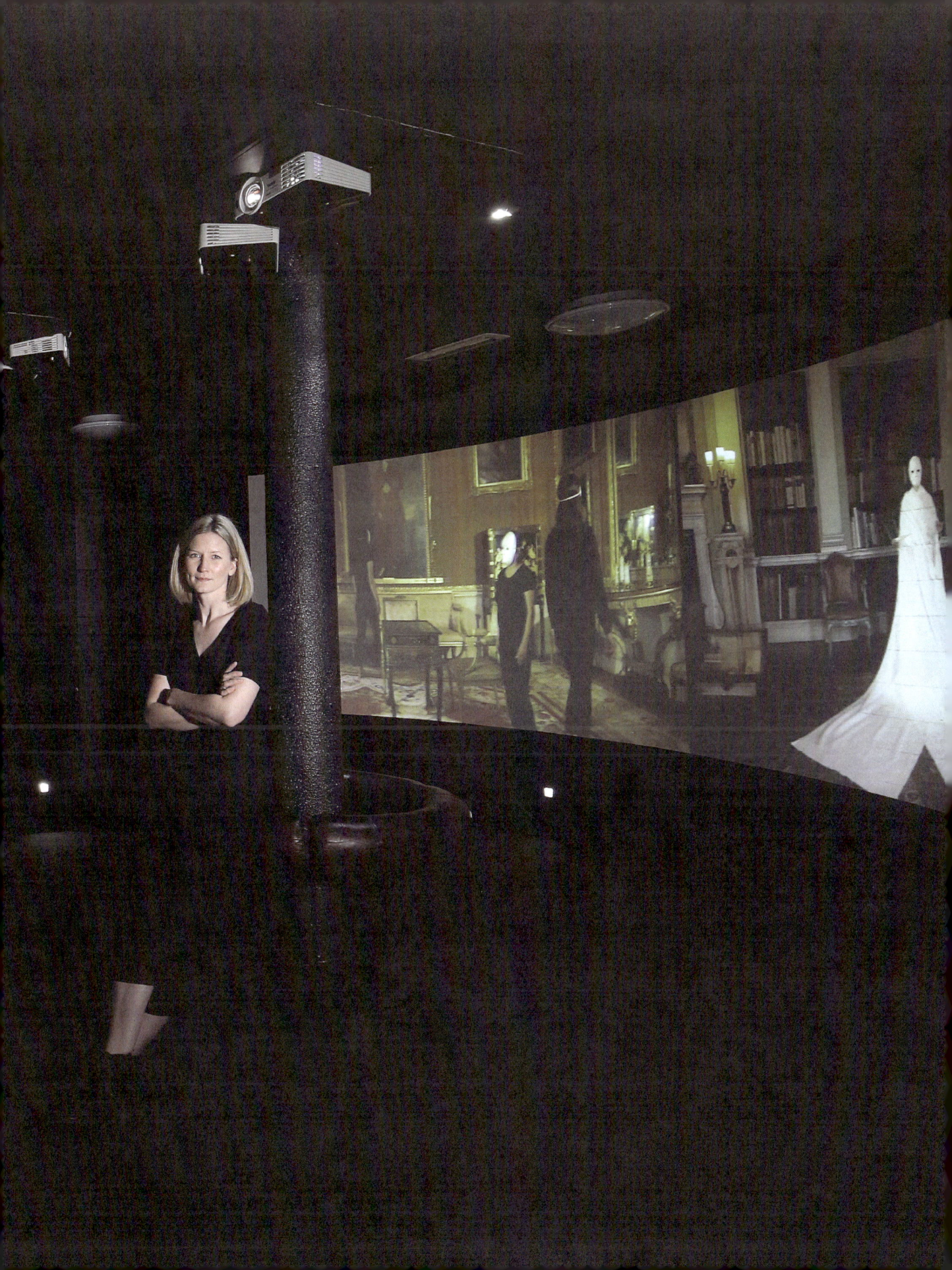

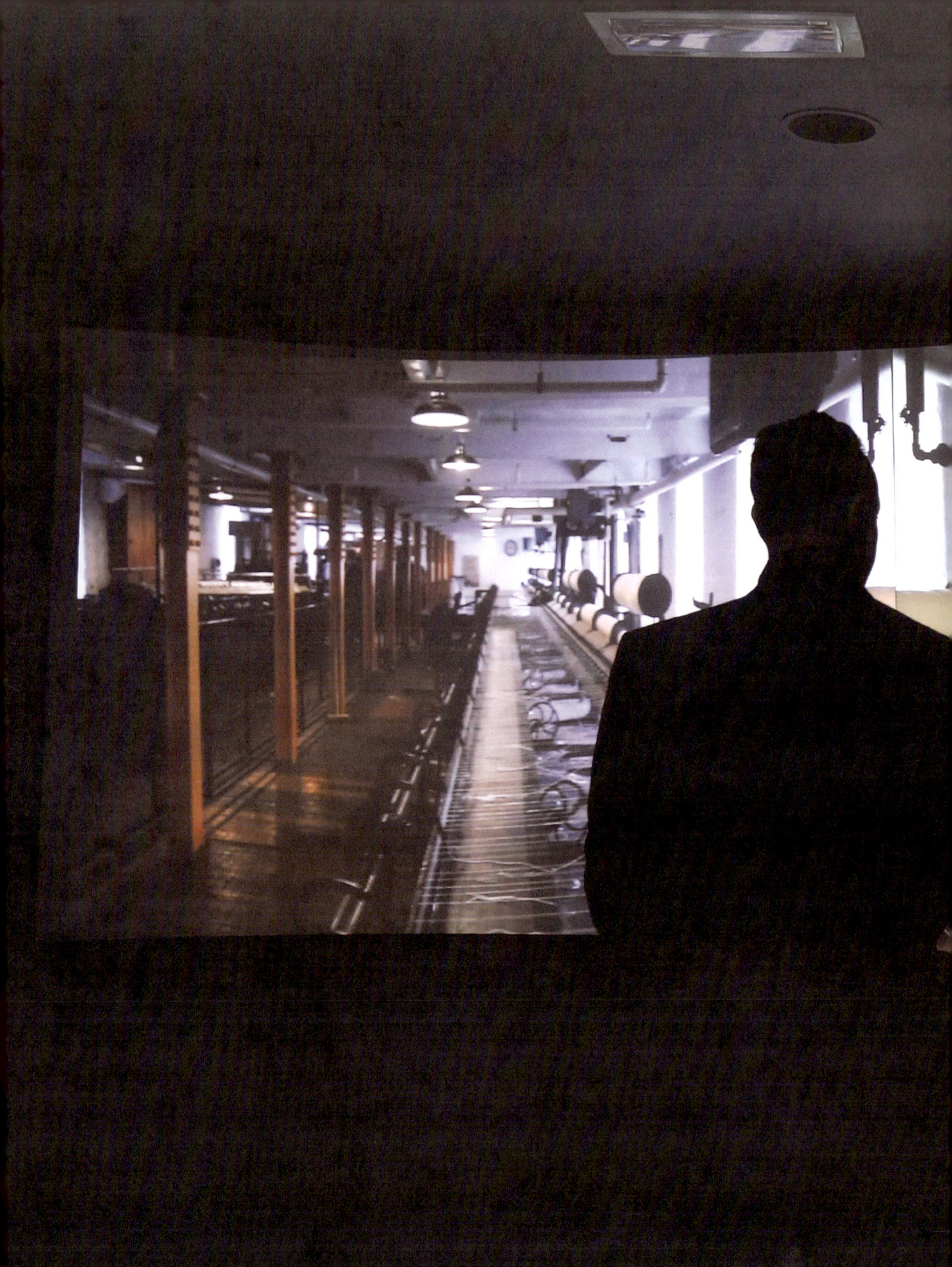

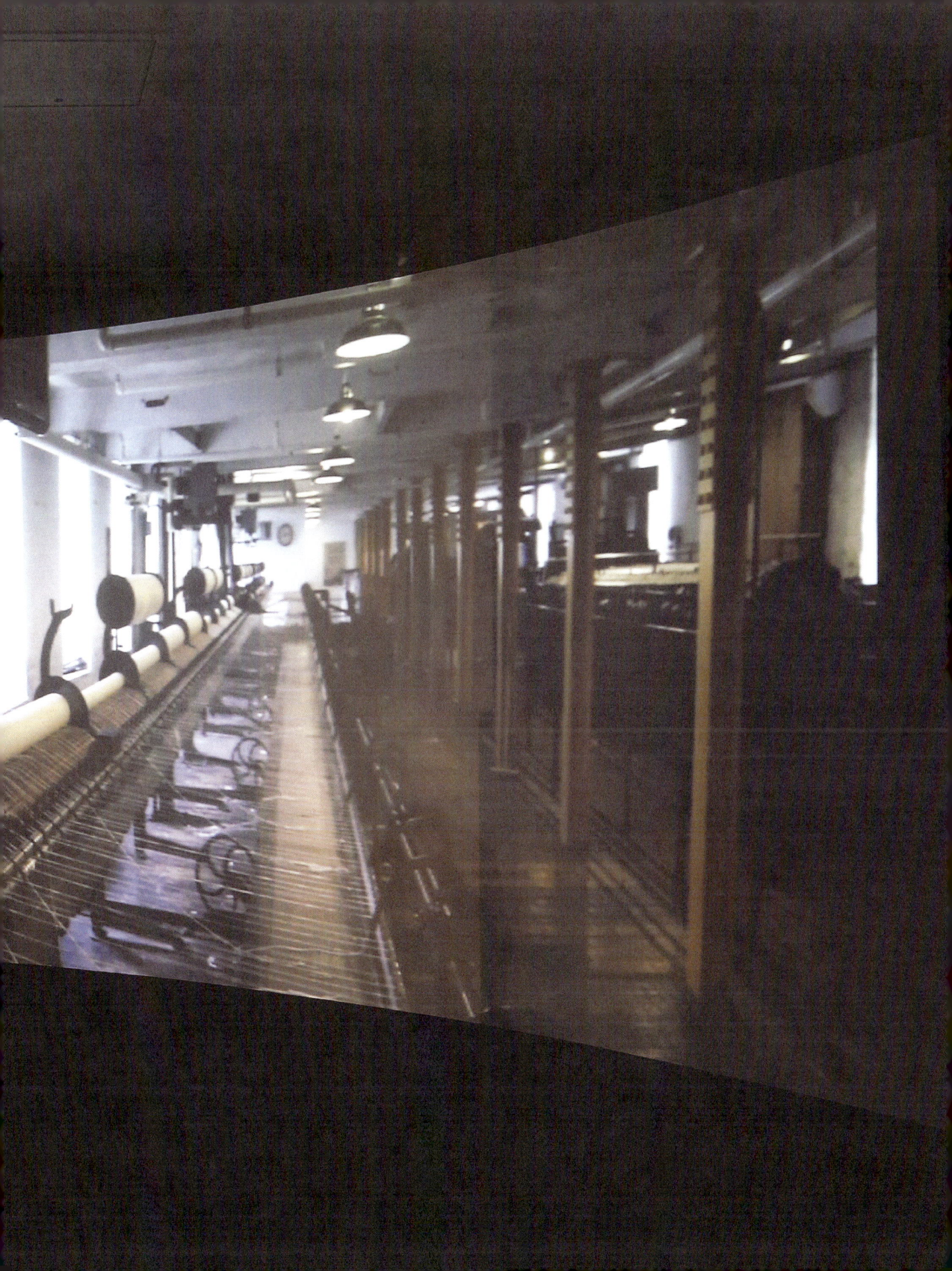

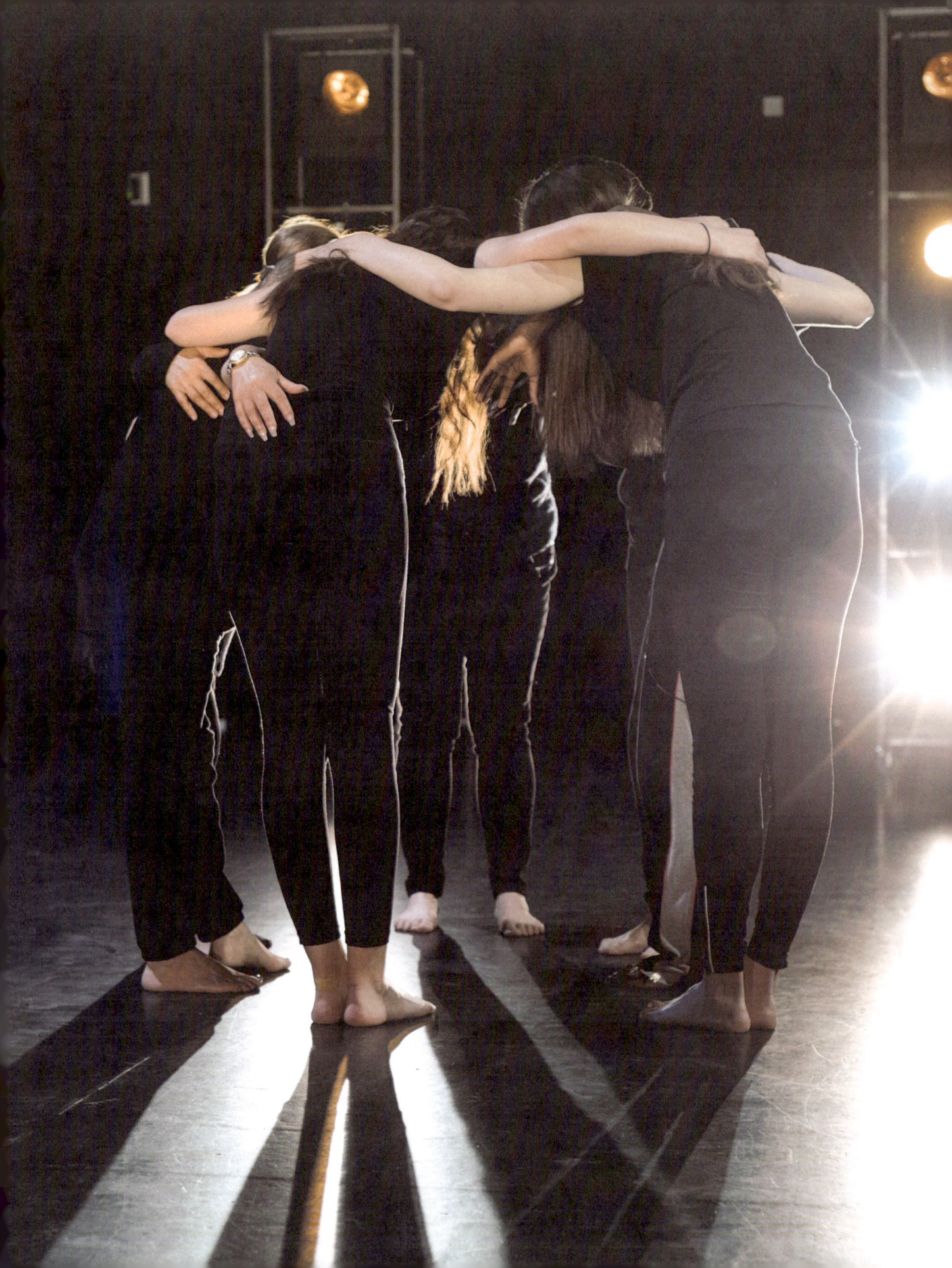

Am I not a woman and a sister
By Sara Jaspan

For many people living in the UK, it is possible to feel distanced from the history of slavery. To view the trade in human flesh only as something terrible that took place a long time ago on faraway shores. As something that holds little relevance to our lives today.

Sadly, this perception is false.

Modern Britain was founded upon wealth generated by the transatlantic slave trade, the legacy of which lives on, tightly interwoven with the material and social fabric of our society. It lingers on our streets named after rich plantation owners. It resides within the walls of many of our top universities, banks and other major institutions, whose investors made their money through slave ownership. It haunts the family lineage of our current and former leaders, such as David Cameron. It underpins our sustained culture of racism and structural inequality.

That this history has been so easily overlooked is no accident. It has been obscured historically by euphemisms such as 'plantation owner' and 'West Indies merchant'. Just as it is overshadowed in current public discourse by the emphasis on Britain's role in bringing about abolition. Abolition, rather than the preceding 270-year-period during which it was one of the leading slave-trading nations. Or the £20m (£2.4bn in today's money) it awarded to 47,000 slave-owning British citizens in 1833 in compensation for their – eventually – liberated 'property'. Taxpayers were still repaying the loan taken out by the government to cover the financial sum up until 2015.

Slavery also continues to play a part in our lives in another invisible way. A report published by the global slavery index estimated that around 136,000 people in the UK were living as slaves in 2017 and that £14bn worth of imported goods (mostly laptops, mobile phones and clothing) were likely to have been made using slave labour. In fact, modern slavery has become a pervasive, if largely undetected, presence within British society, fuelled by the same consumerist demands and ingrained system of global wealth inequality first created by the transatlantic slave trade centuries ago.

Artist Elizabeth Kwant's 13-minute-long looping film installation, *Am I not a woman and a sister* (2019), asks us to quietly acknowledge and bear witness to these uncomfortable realities. It was co-created with female survivors of modern slavery trafficked to the UK and uses objects, gestures, locations and sounds that relate to the transatlantic slave trade and its particular connection with the North West of England. (The region from where tens of thousands of ships once departed for Africa to trade goods for people, where imported slave-produced cotton was woven in countless textile factories, and where significant wealth was accrued as a result). In this way, Kwant's piece collapses the time-space distance between slavery past and present, bringing the two into dialogue and re-inscribing forgotten legacies back onto the British landscape.

Acknowledging such connections is important. How else can we hope to fully engage with some of the most deep-rooted problems of our time or disrupt history's reoccurring patterns?

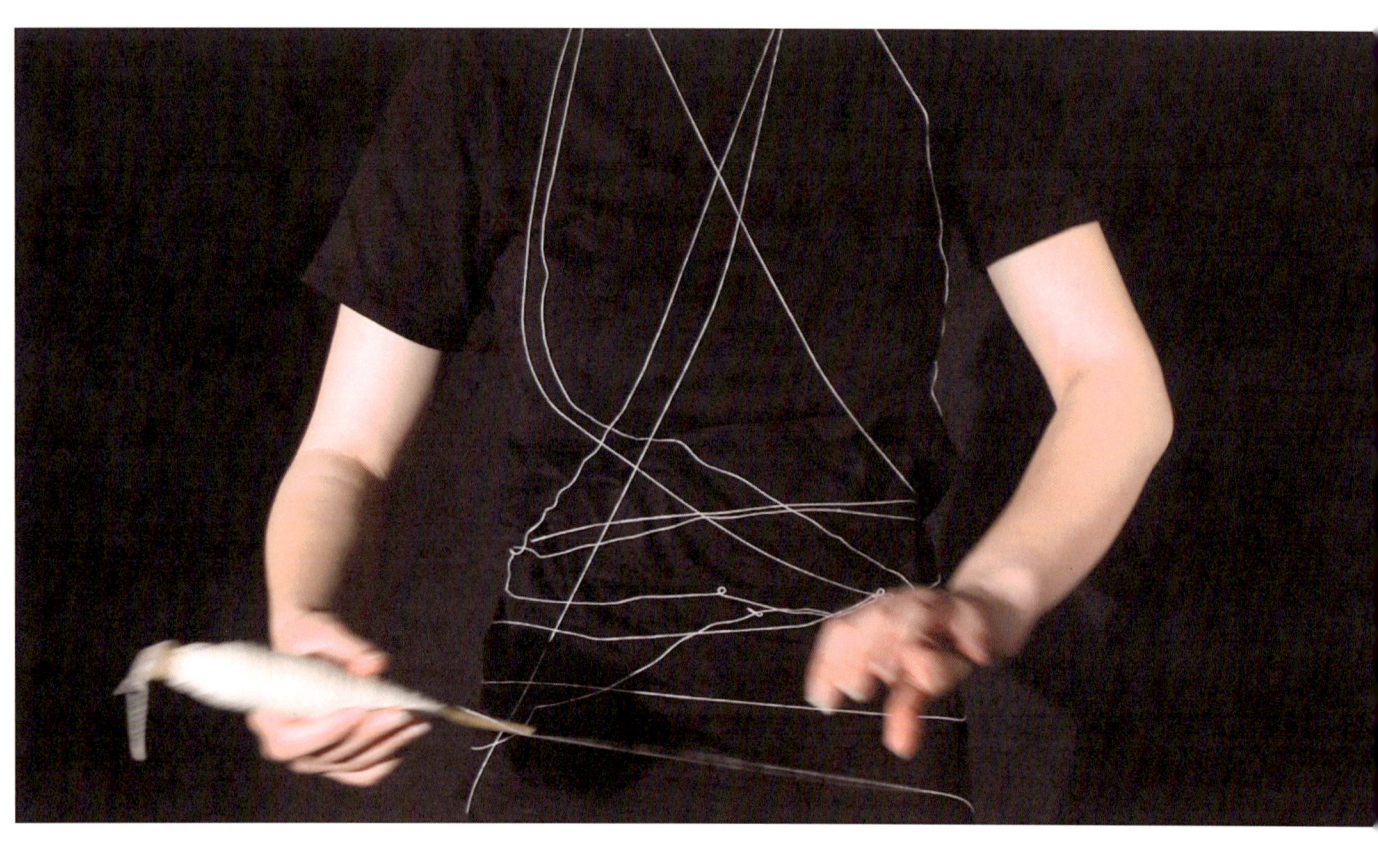

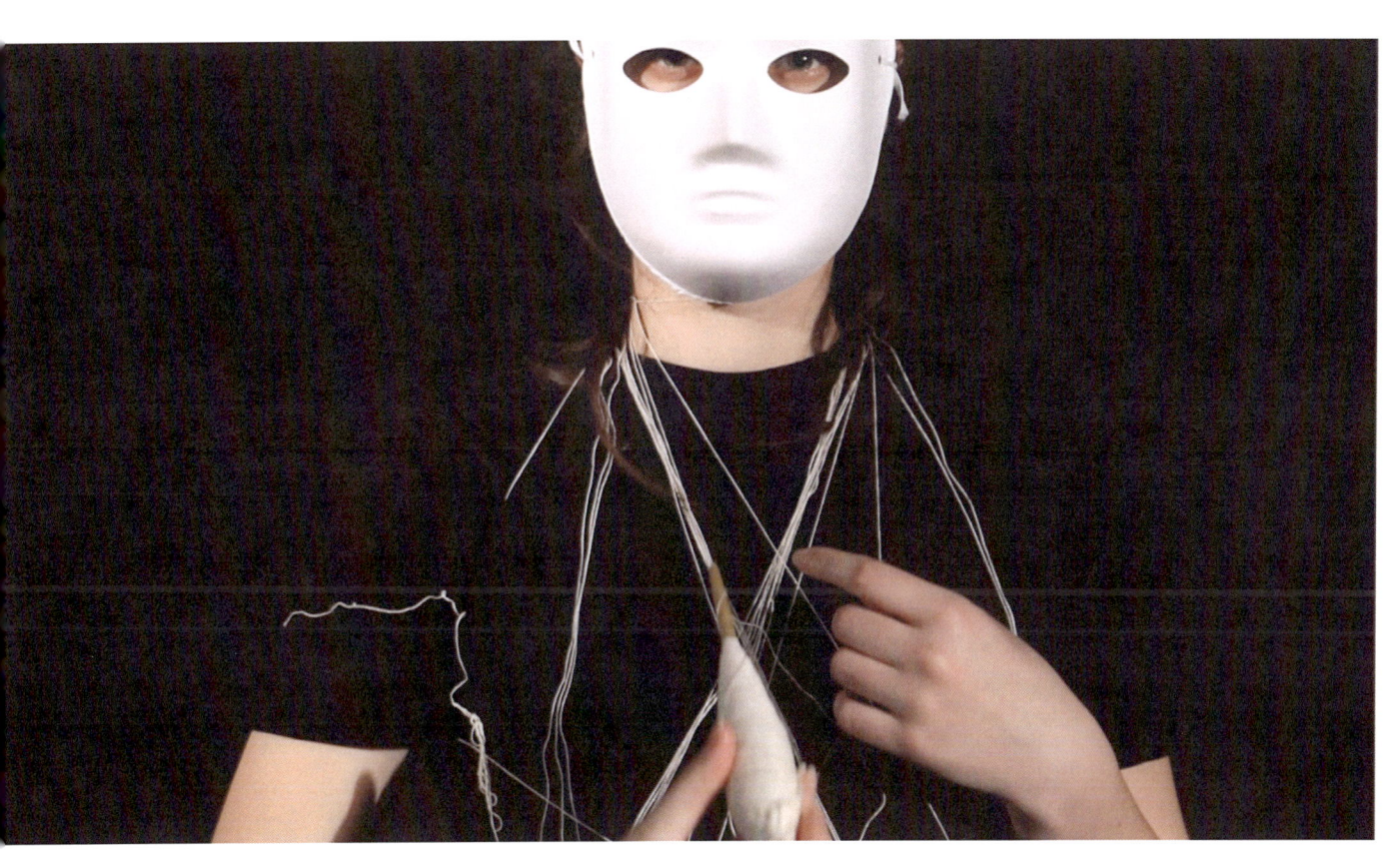

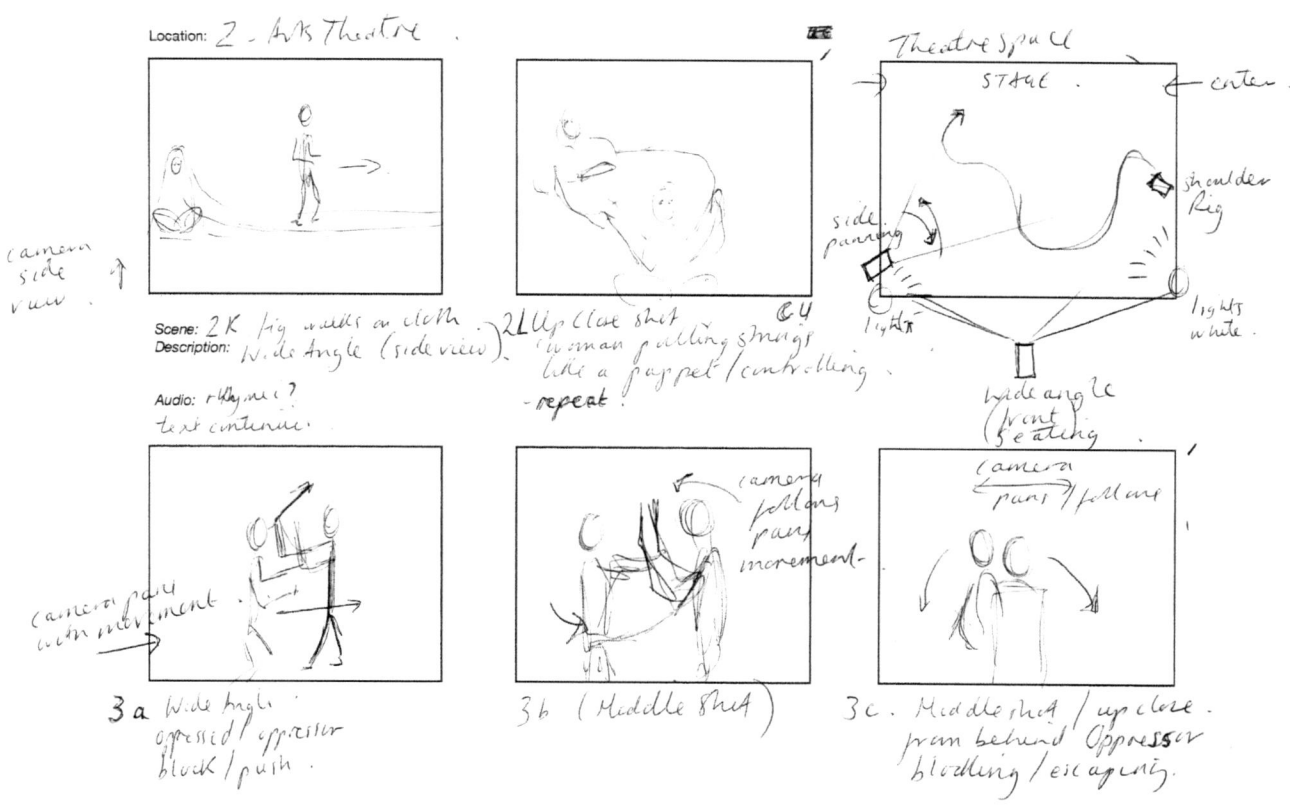

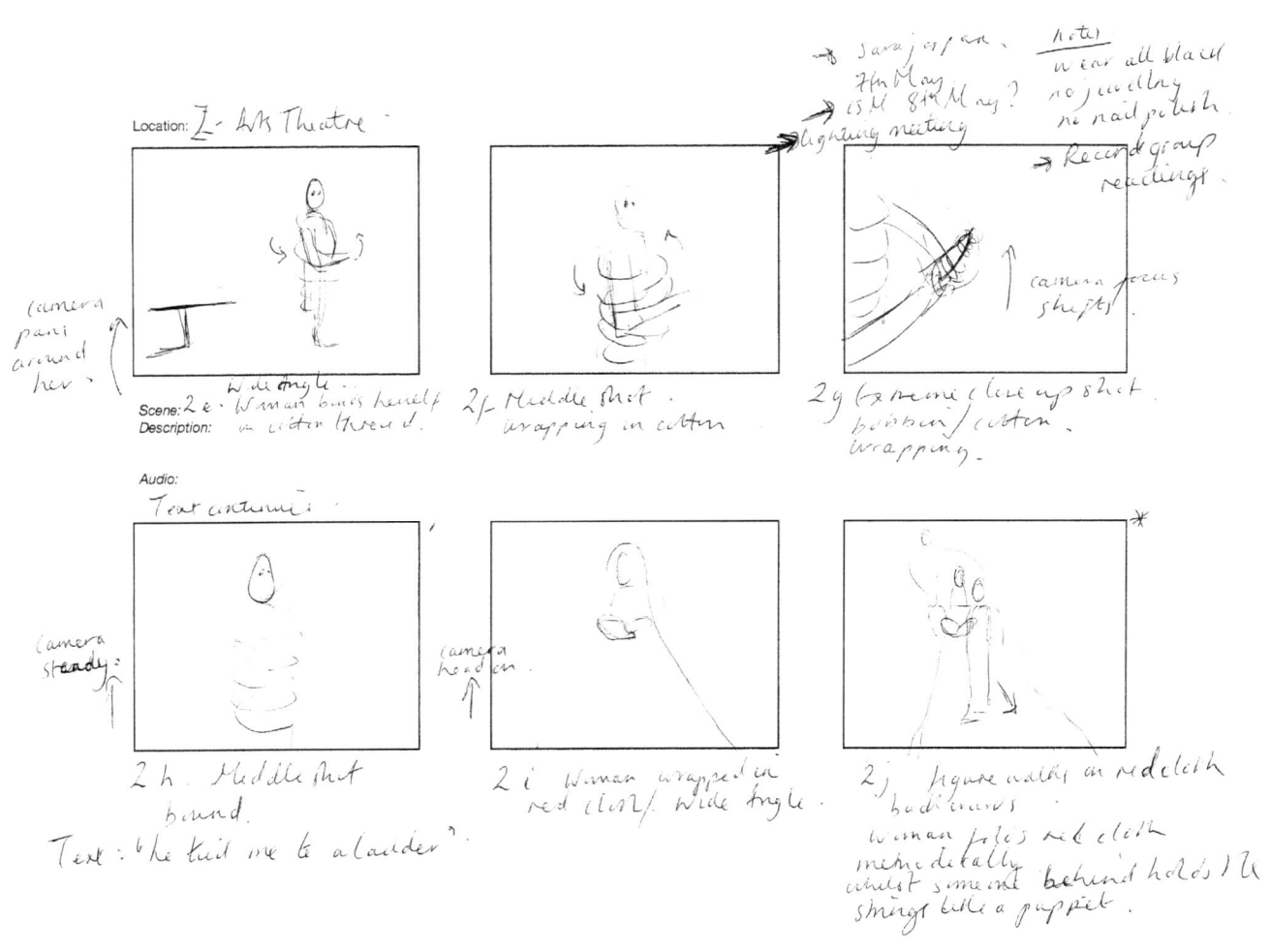

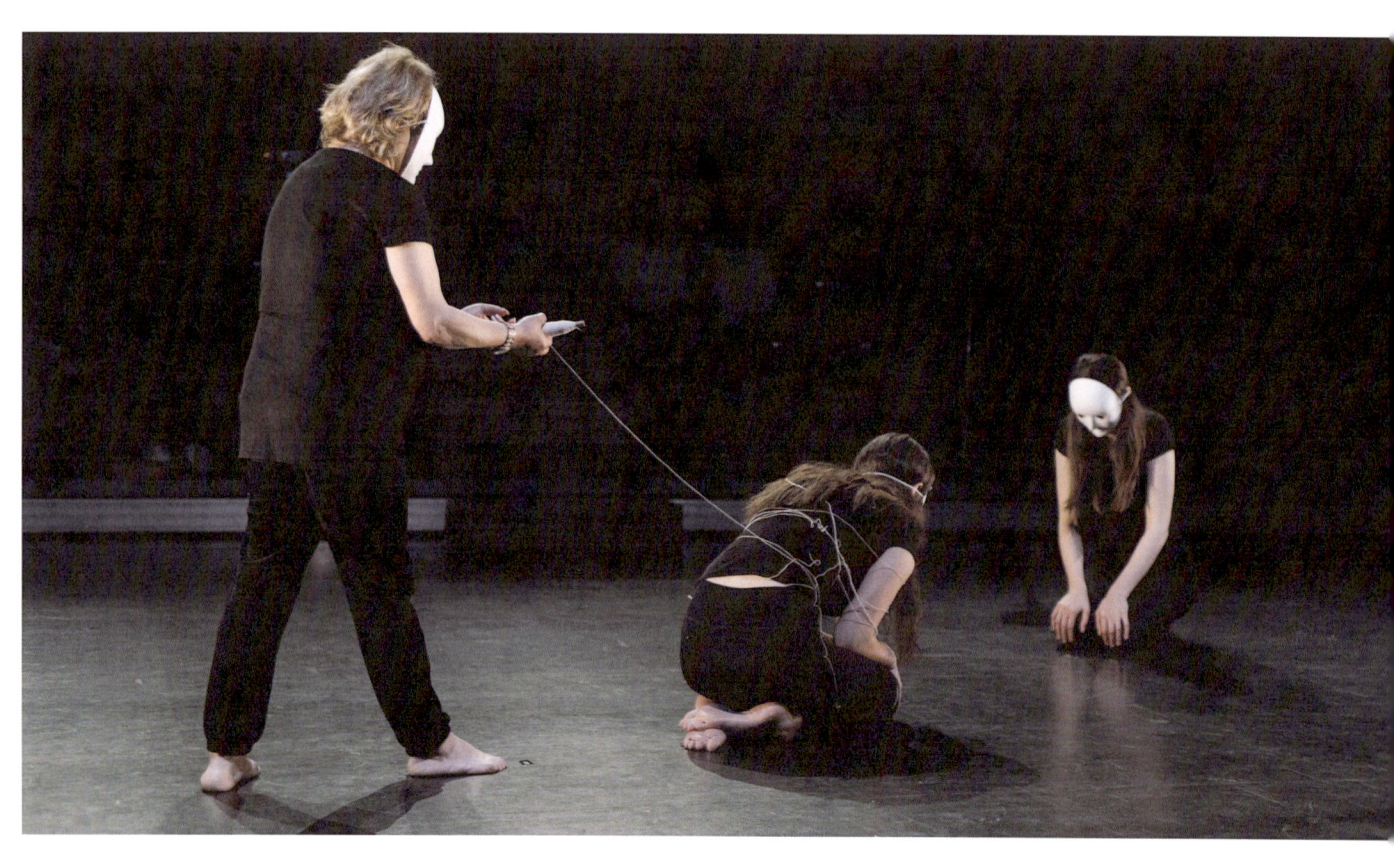

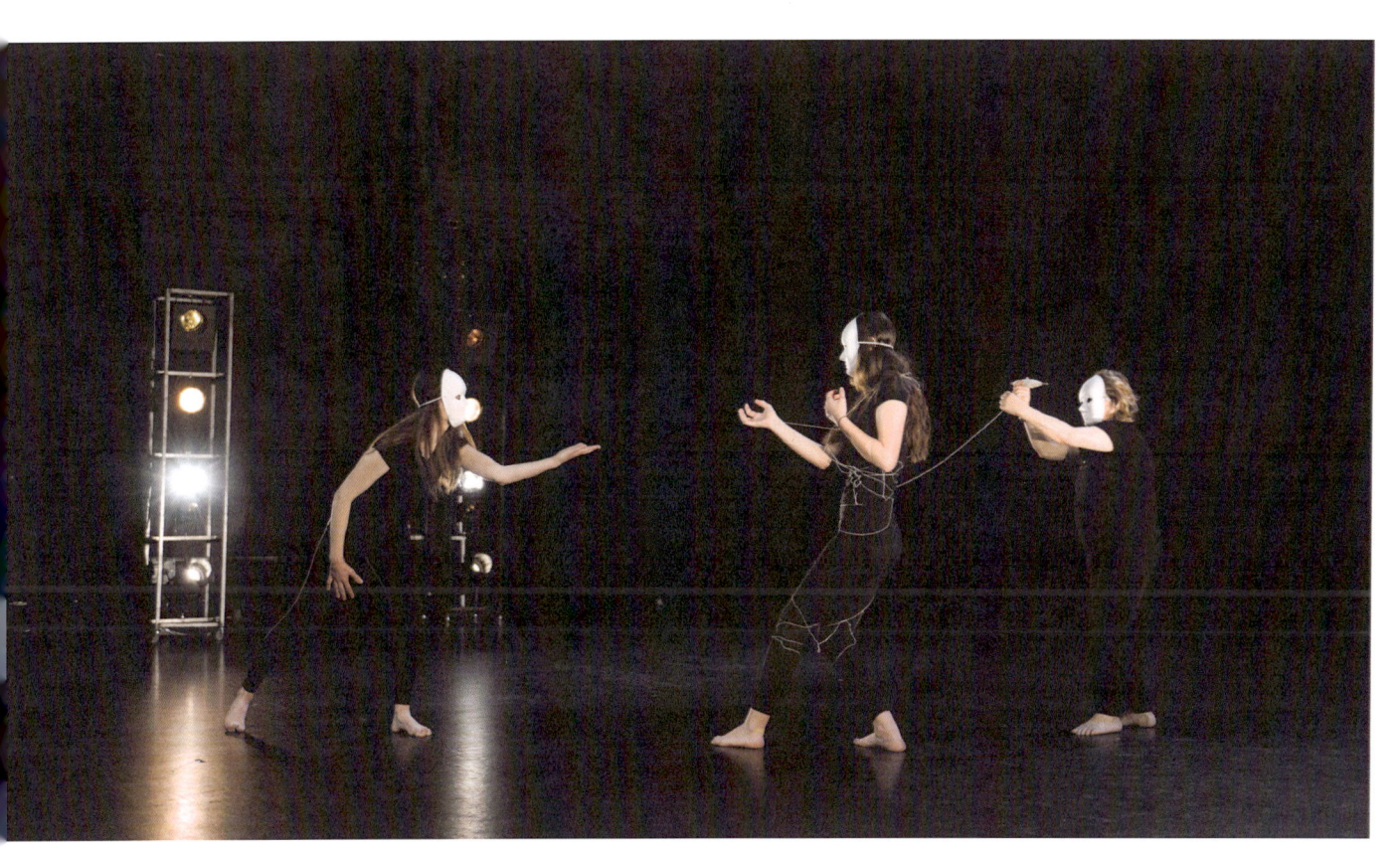

Kwant has engaged directly with issues of migration, immigration, legacies of colonialism, and modern slavery throughout her practice. For example, her project *In-Transit* (2018) took the form of a series of site-specific performances in which she physically embodied positions adopted by people journeying along the primary western migration route into Europe. Poignantly, several of the poses echo the corpse-like position forced upon enslaved Africans held below deck during the deadly Middle Passage.

In recent years, the artist has grown increasingly interested in the ability of movement to convey story and its therapeutic potential as a mechanism for processing trauma. The actions and gestures in *Am I not a woman and a sister* were devised by the women in the film during a series of workshops facilitated by Kwant and British Barbadian choreographer Magdalen Bartlett Luambia (whose family history is inextricably linked with slavery). They are based on their personal experiences of oppression, survival and recovery – as well as their response to the transatlantic slave trade.

The performed movements occur within a blacked-out studio space and in the lavish Cinnamon Room and Old Library of Harewood House, a large country home near Leeds built between 1759-1771 for the wealthy plantation and slave owner Edwin Lascelles, 1st Baron Harewood. The other important location in the piece is Quarry Bank – a Lancashire cotton mill established in 1784 by the Greg family, who also owned slaves and several sugar plantations in the Caribbean.

One of the most striking scenes that we encounter centres on a lone woman, draped in a train of pristine white cloth. She stands silently before us in a manner that mirrors the iconography of Lady Justice – except that her sword and set of scales have been replaced with a spool of white cotton, which she holds in one hand, wrapping the length of its thread around the fingers of her other in a continuous gesture. Her blindfold is missing, too. Instead, a piercing set of eyes stare out from behind a blank white mask, momentarily interlocking with our own; confronting the viewer. Preventing us from looking away.

All of the women in the film wear masks. Partly to protect their identity (though they have each escaped their former enslavement, they remain at risk). But the dehumanising effect adds another layer of significance; resonating with the degrees of separation, alienation and othering that have always been fundamental to the denial of humanity and mistreatment of others. The historic depiction of African people as 'savage' or 'animal-like' helped legitimise their reduction to 'black cattle' – to an en-slaveable, money-making commodity for which concern need only extend as far as business profits and loss. Today, political/media rhetoric has branded those fleeing war, persecution and poverty as a threatening mass of anonymous 'migrants' and 'refugees', rather than as fellow beings (a move which helped institute the UK Home Office's hostile environment policy in 2012, contributing to the problem of human trafficking and exploitation).

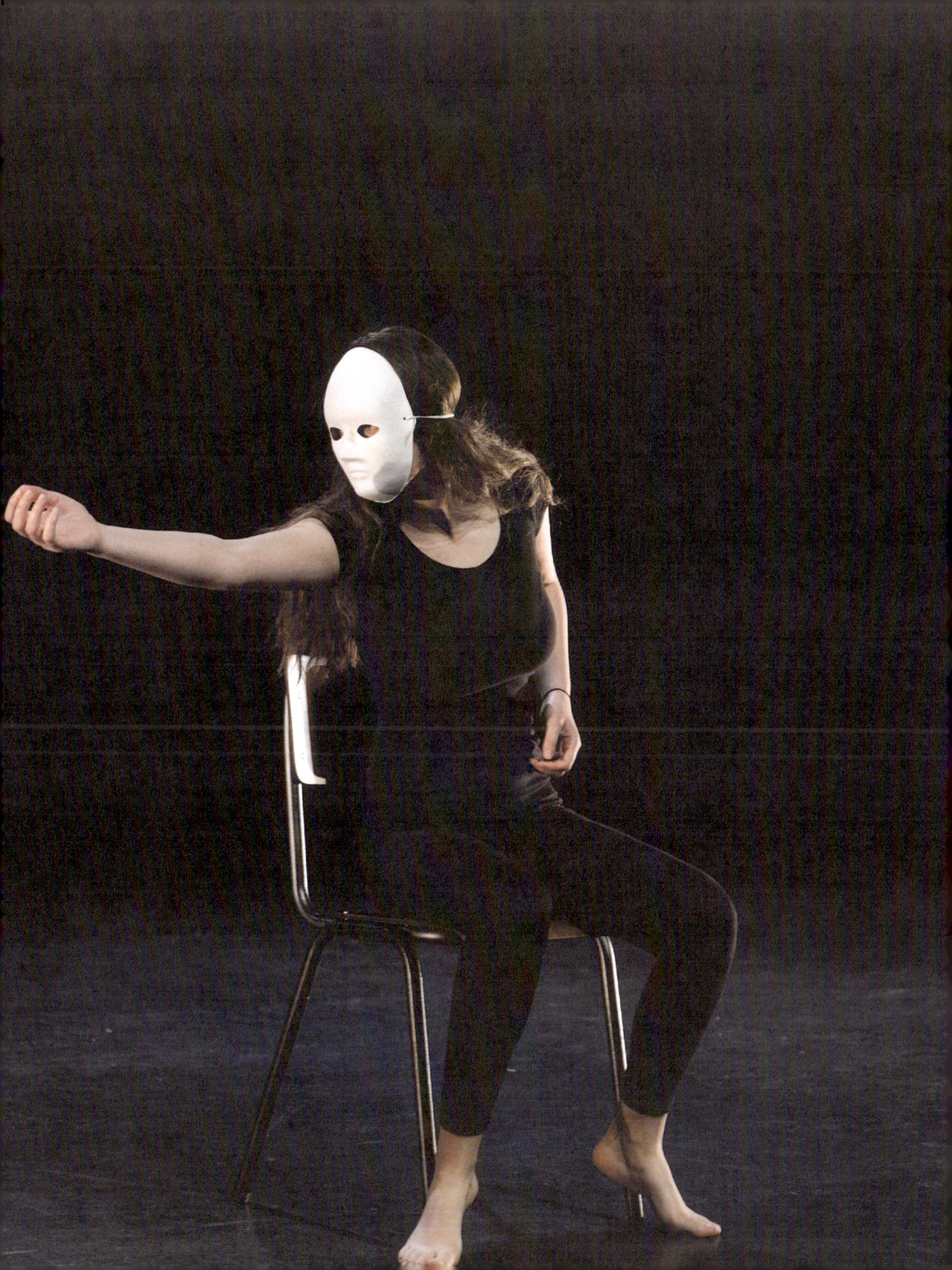

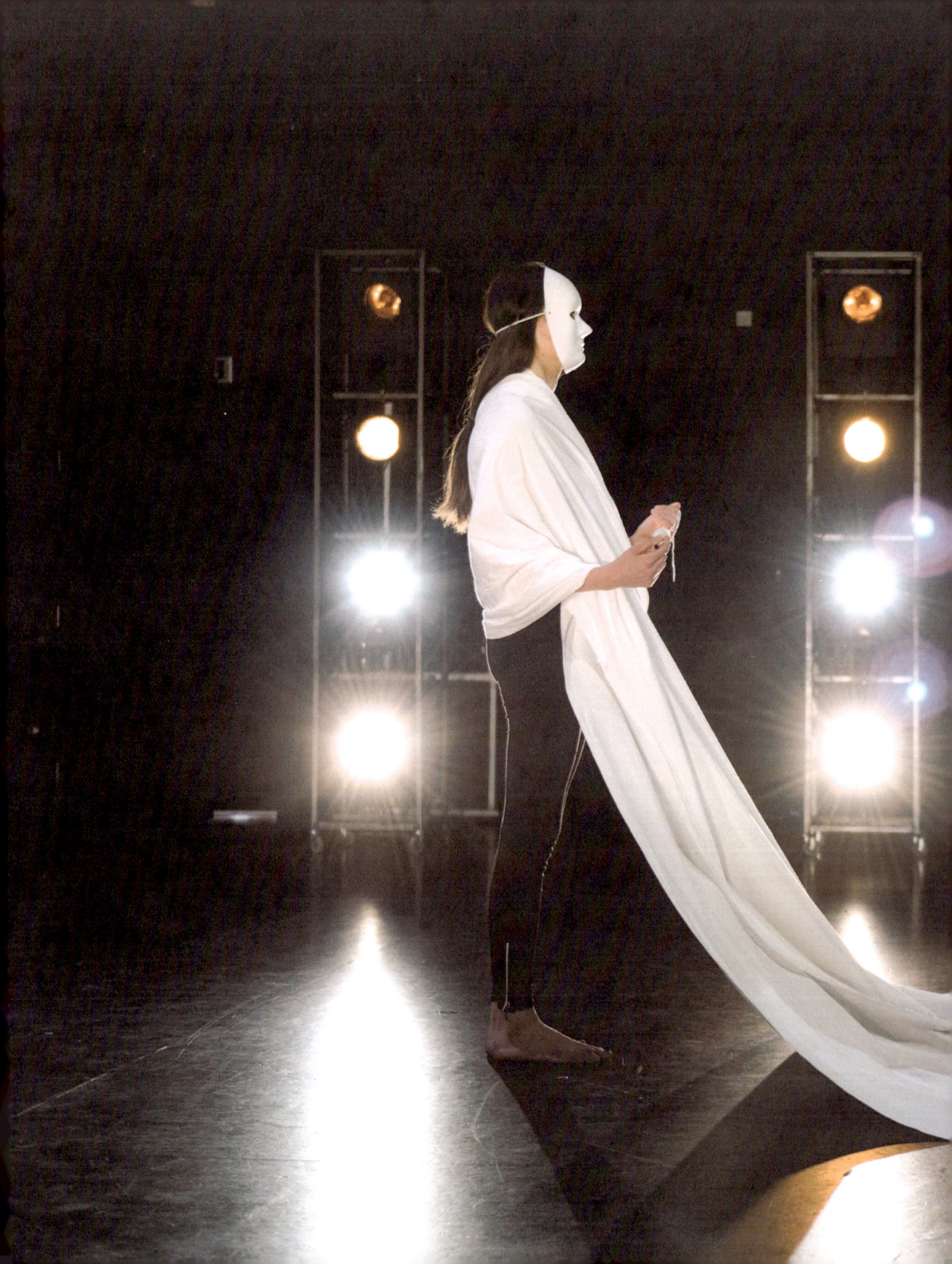

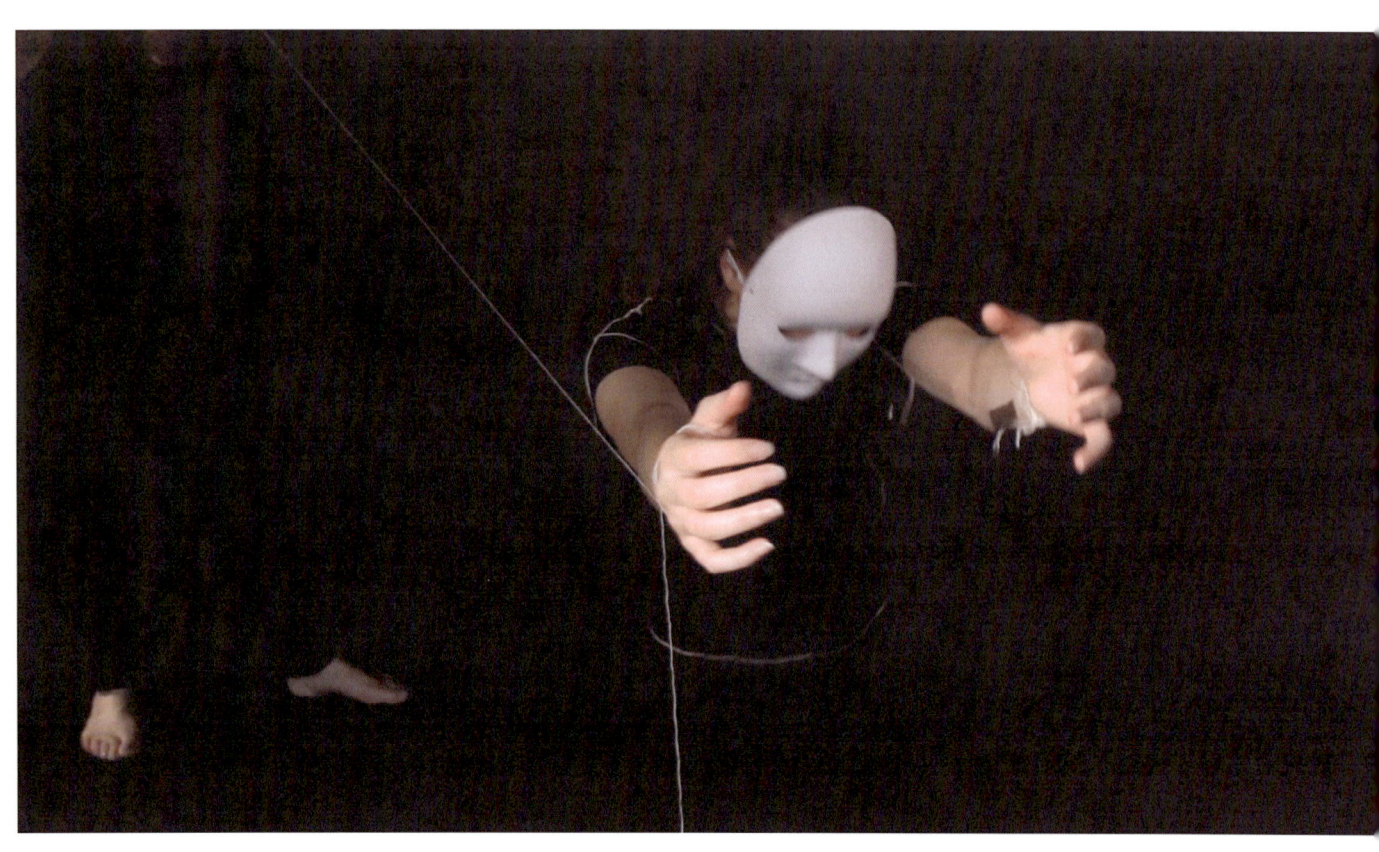

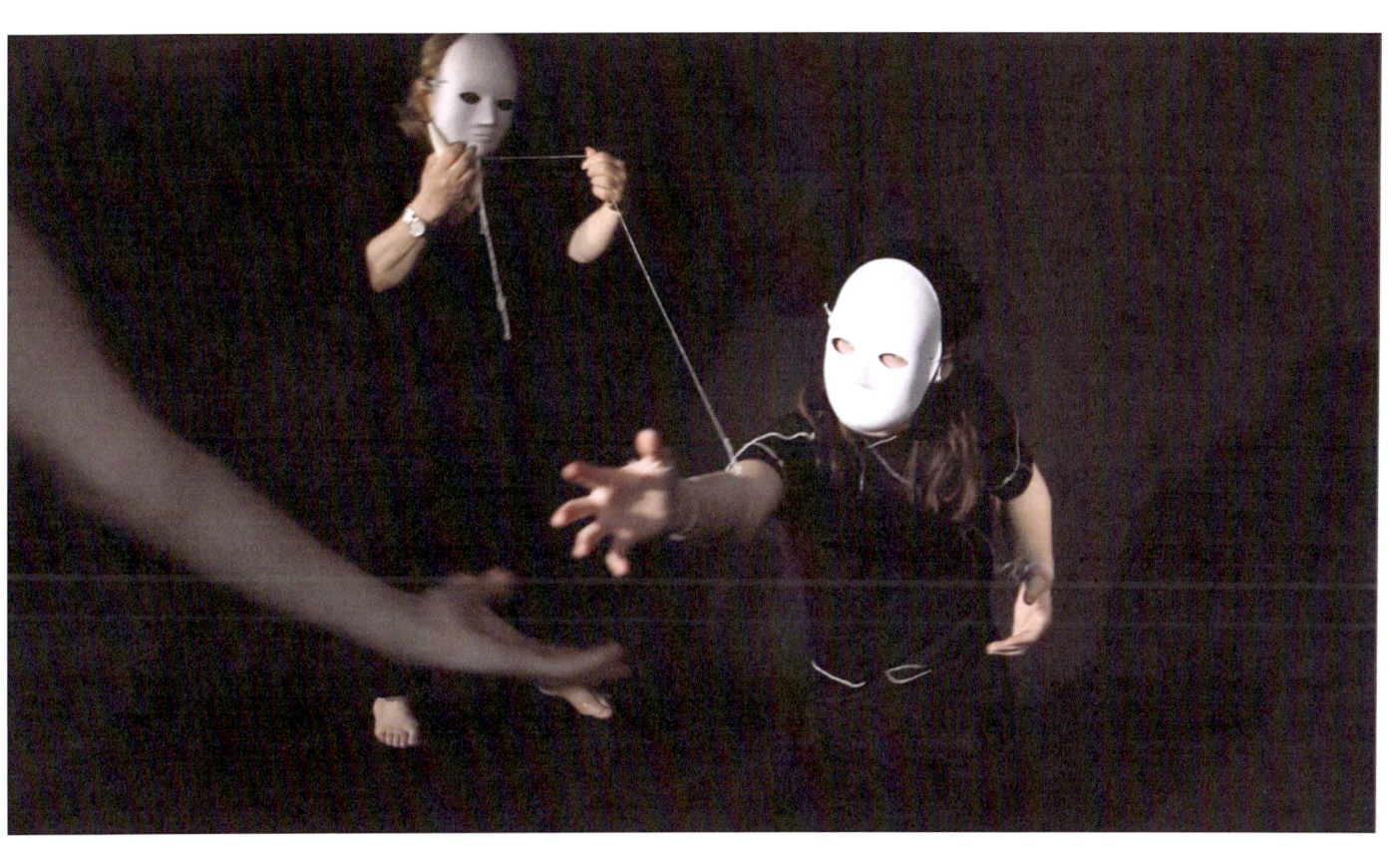

The cotton sheet and spool in this section of the film reappear throughout. Their stark whiteness conjures thoughts relating to the whitewashing of history, and of course the racialised aspect that has long coloured slavery. But these objects also carry additional forms of symbolic cargo. At other points during the piece, we watch a woman slowly folding the infinite length of cloth in upon itself, referencing the reoccurrence of different forms of enslavement throughout humanity's shared past. The bobbin unwinds endlessly as the other performers entangle themselves and each other in ceaseless trails of bondage, domination and oppression. Such impressions are underscored by the soundscape, which features the ticking of a clock, connoting a sense of history, memory and the passage of time; while the ghostly, layered voices of women singing suggest echoes of trauma travelling back across generations.

The sound design was composed by Sarah Sarhandi and features other significant details, like the pounding clatter of the cotton looms at Quarry Bank. This in turn contrasts with the tranquil birdsong, trickling water and harpsichord music accompanying the scenes shot at Harewood, further contributing to the narrative of exhausting toil and hardship serving gentrified leisure.

Am I not a woman and a sister is presented at the International Slavery Museum in Liverpool – once the largest slave trade port in the Atlantic world – not far from a window overlooking sites where slave ships bound for Africa docked to load goods and for repair. The permanent gallery collection surrounding Kwant's installation includes shackles, manacles, whips and other original artefacts of subjugation and violence used against enslaved African people, shown alongside displays detailing the abject conditions of the Middle Passage. The film itself is highly immersive, projected across four curved screens that encircle the viewer. The combined effect of witnessing both the artwork and the history it references within such close proximity is deeply powerful.

Another source of the work's power comes simply from its title. The historic phrase originates from a series of copper tokens commissioned by the American Anti-Slavery Society in New York in 1837, the design of which was based on Josiah Wedgwood's 'Am I Not a Man And a Brother?' anti-slavery medallion but substituted the enslaved man for a woman. The switch not only reflected a growing concern for the forms of sexual exploitation experienced by female African American slaves during the period, but also highlighted the prominent role that women were playing in the antislavery movement.

The broader resonance of these words has allowed them to transcend their time and social context, however, and continue to be applied in other campaigns for justice and equality. At their most basic level, they present nothing but a demand for our shared humanity to be seen and not denied. They find their equivalent in the women's steady gaze as they stare out from behind their masks into the camera; returning the viewer's own. *Am I not a woman and a sister* is a call to bear witness to the legacies of slavery past and confront its existence within the present, without which, how can real change and healing ever begin?

Sara Jaspan is a freelance writer and editor based in Manchester.

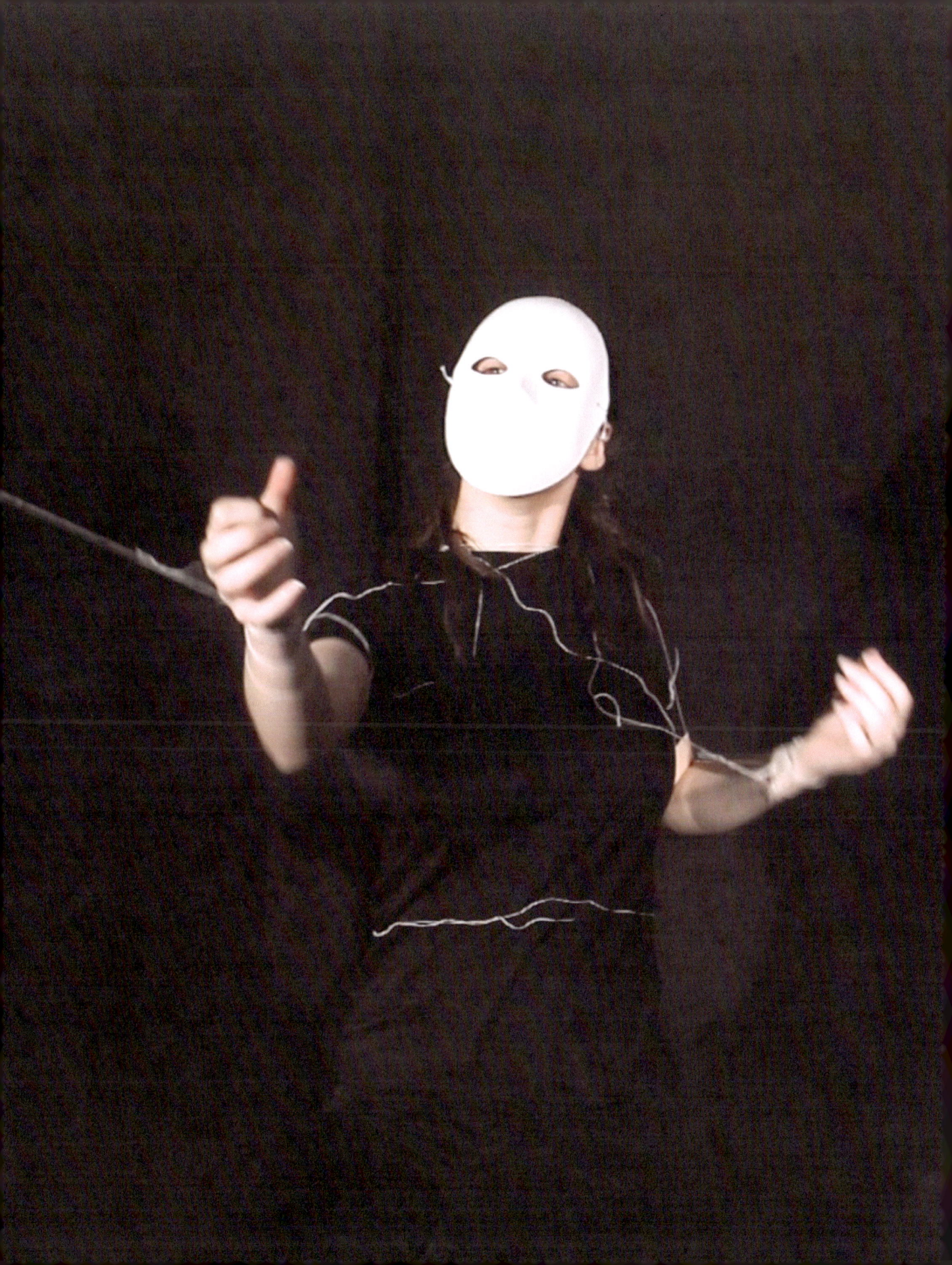

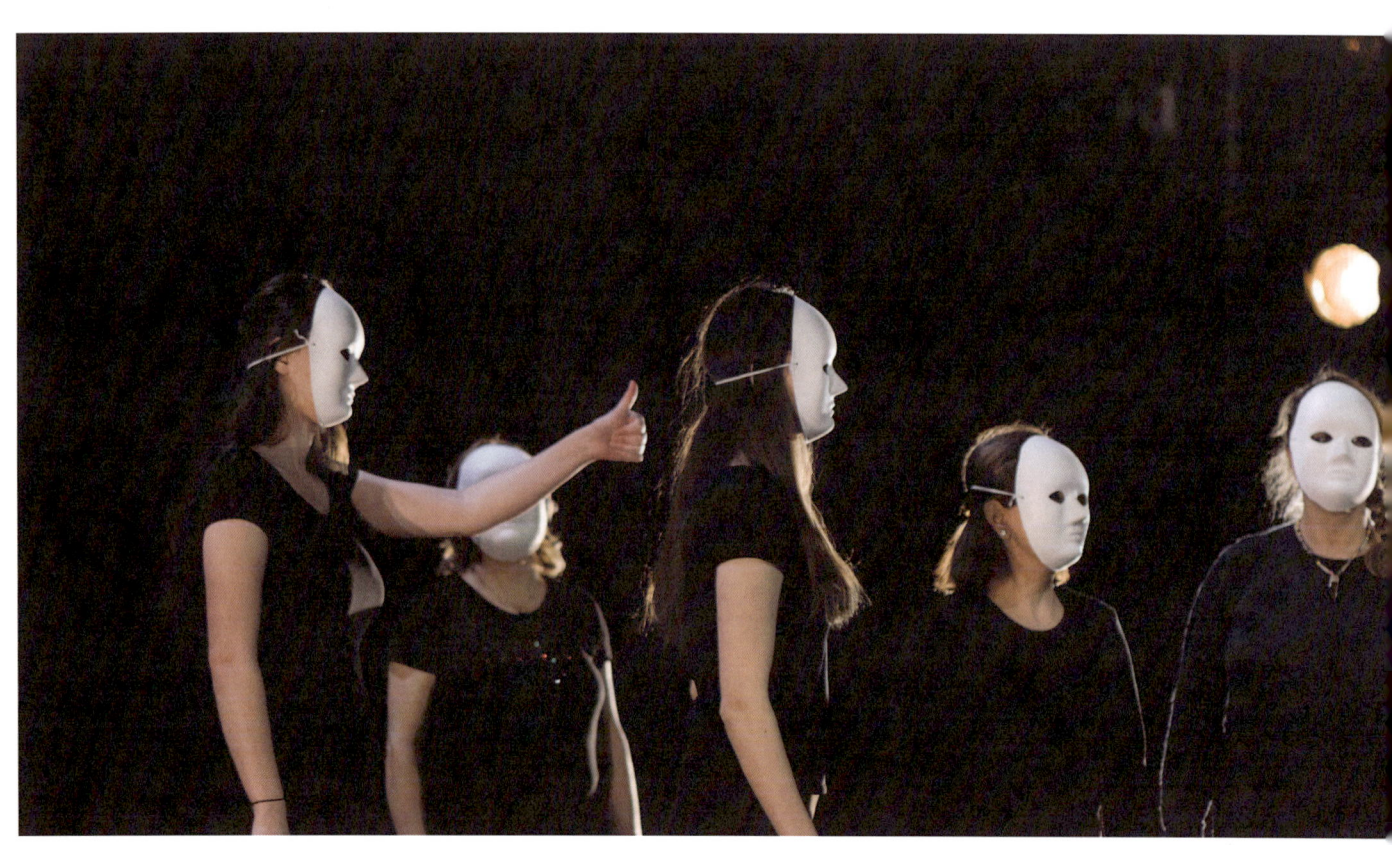

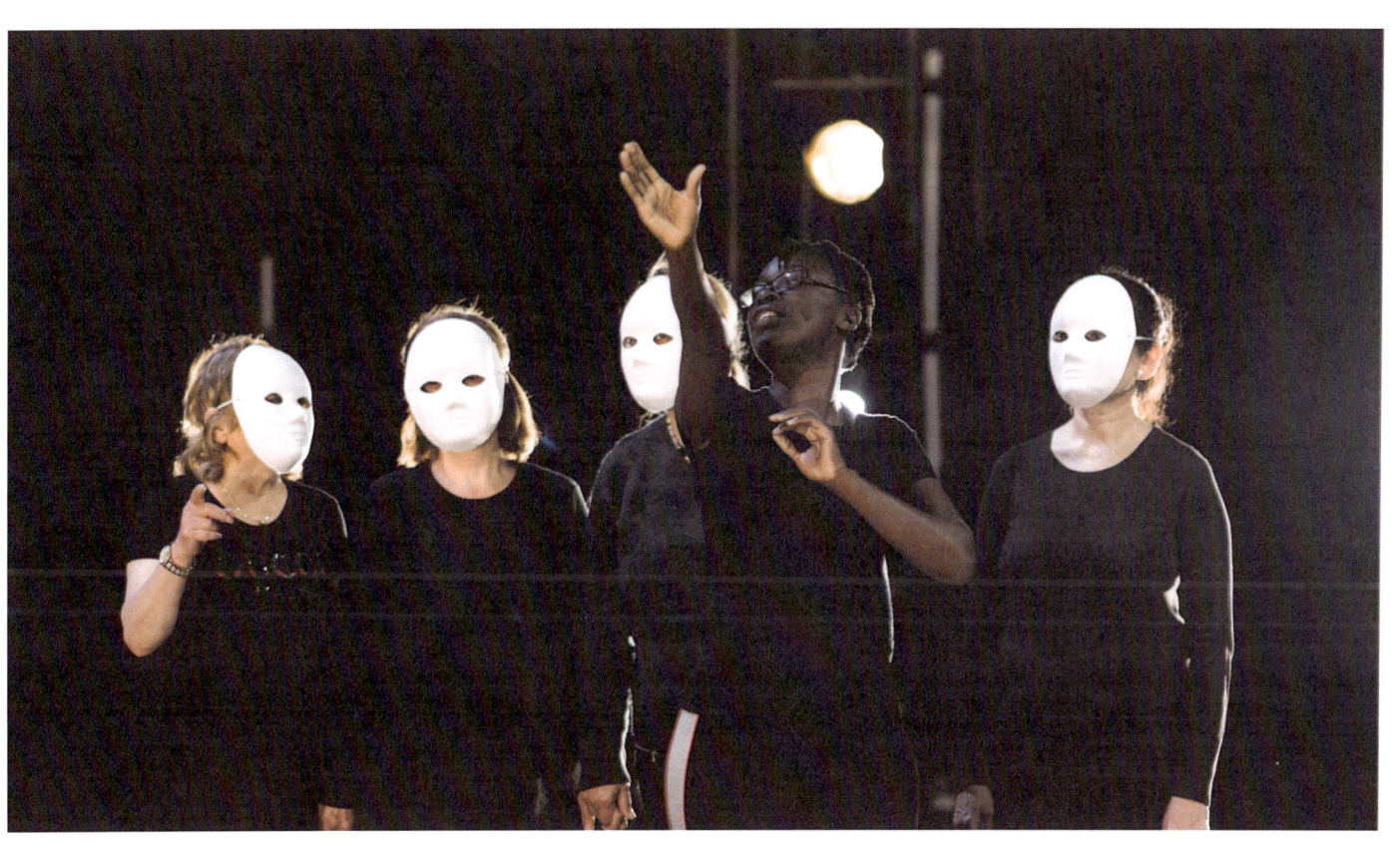

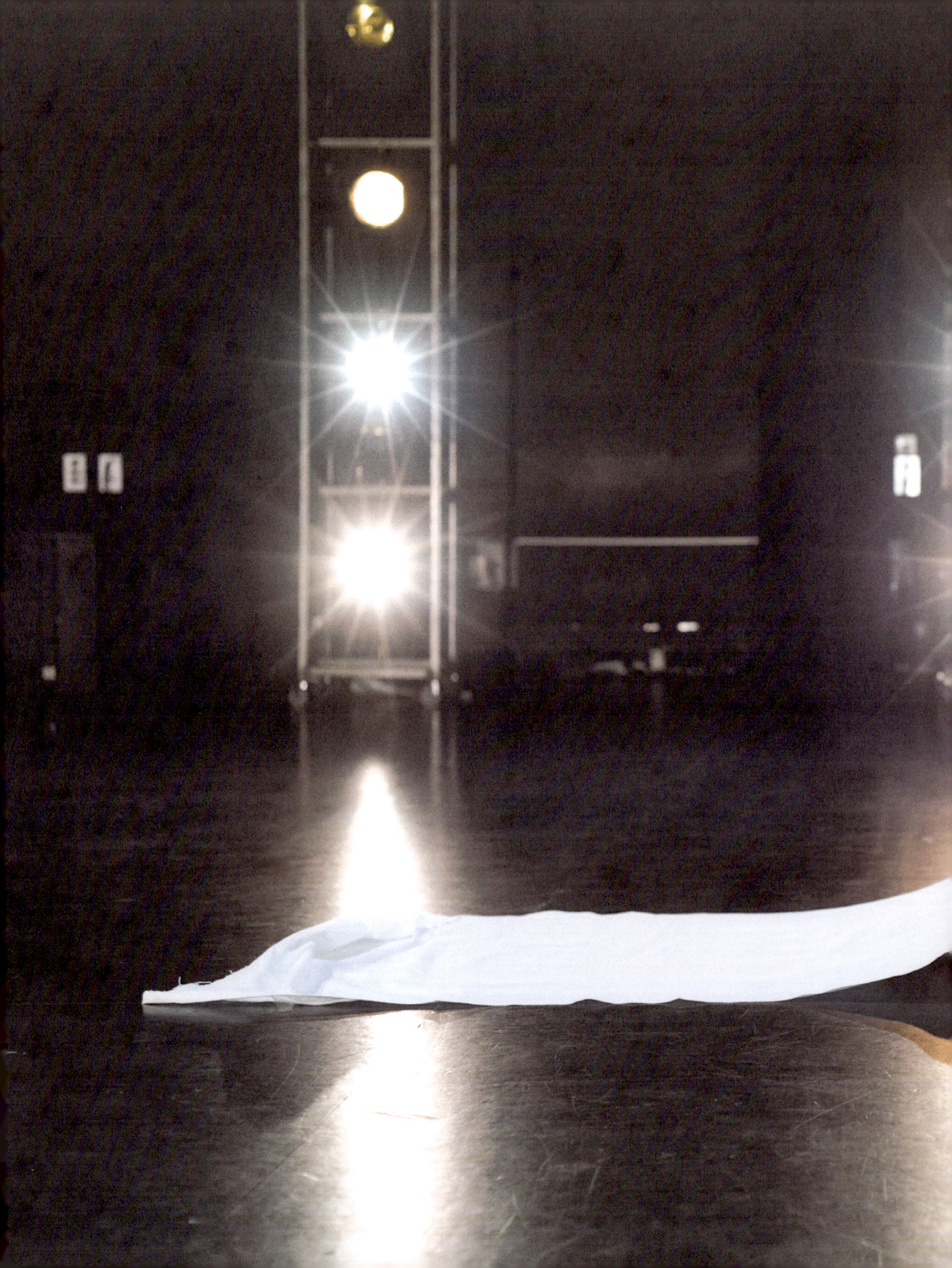

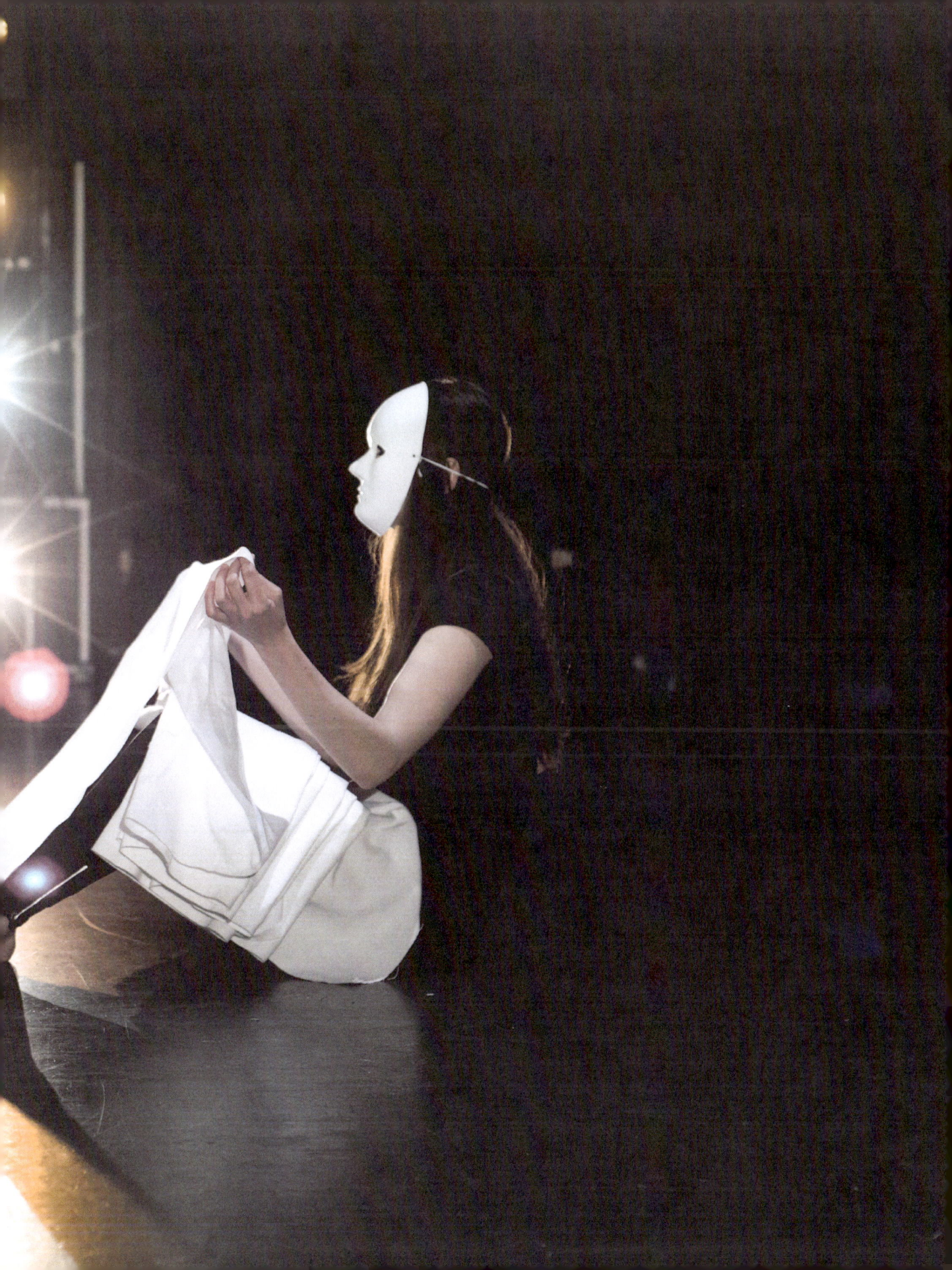

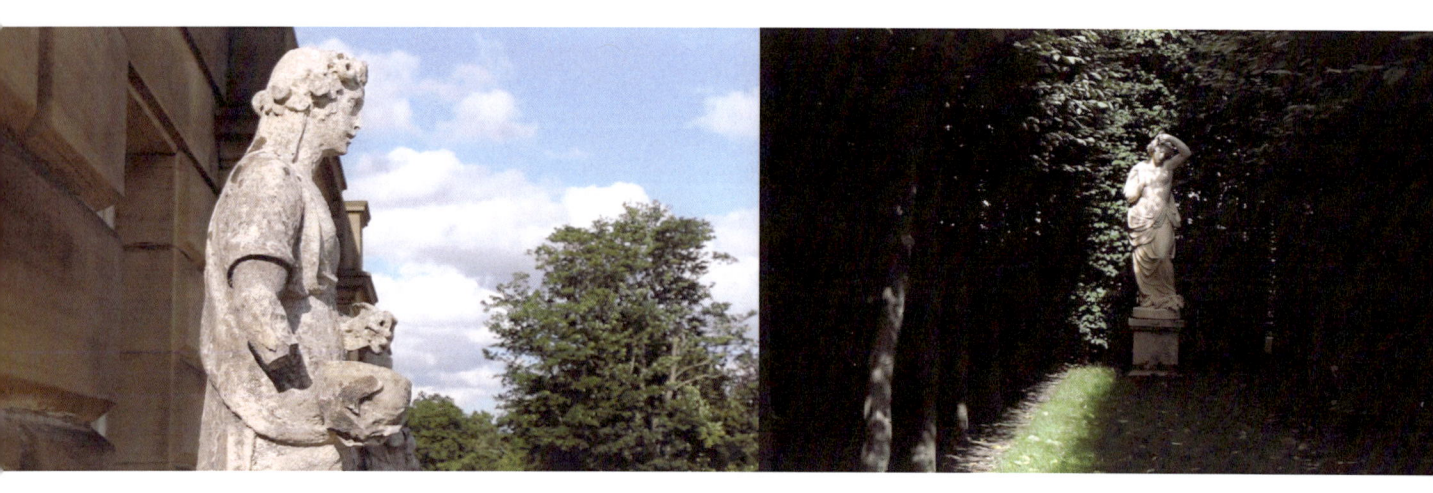

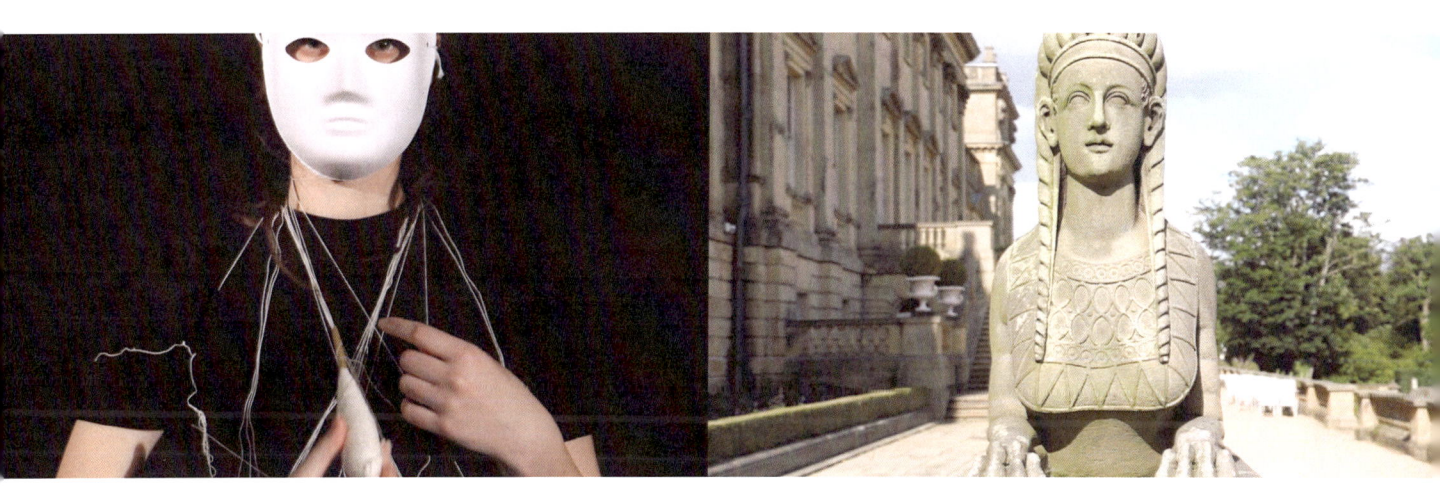

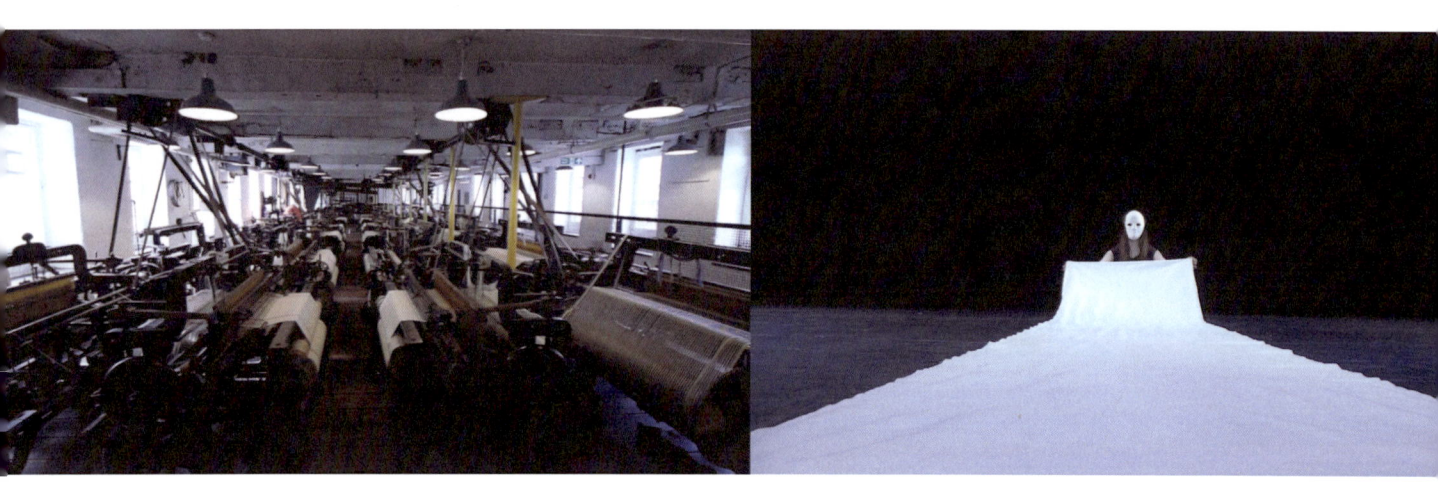

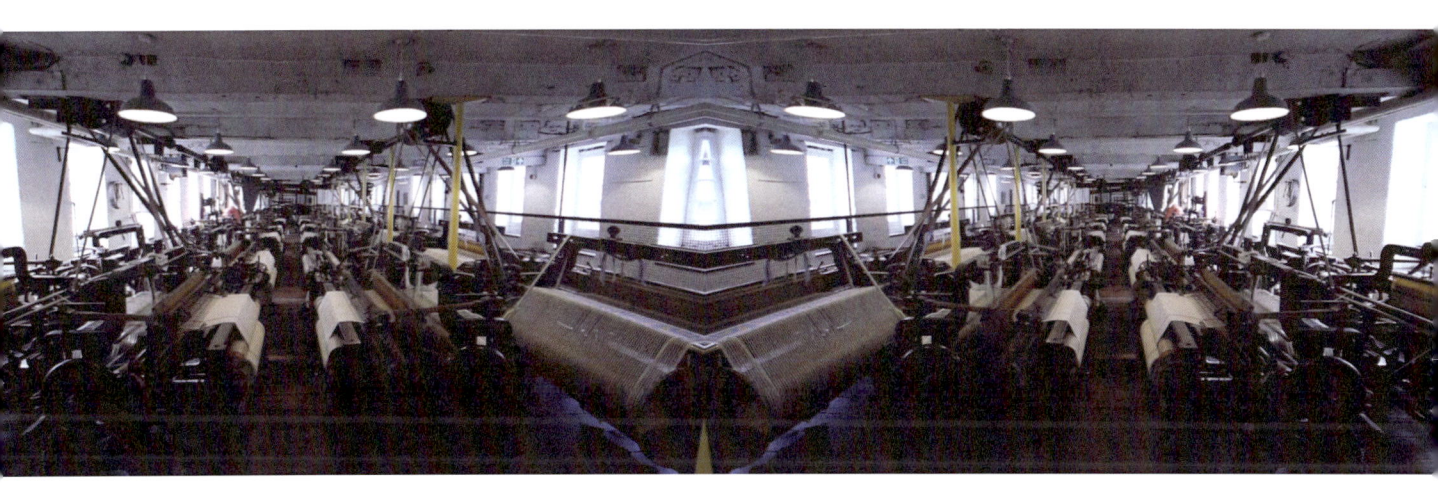

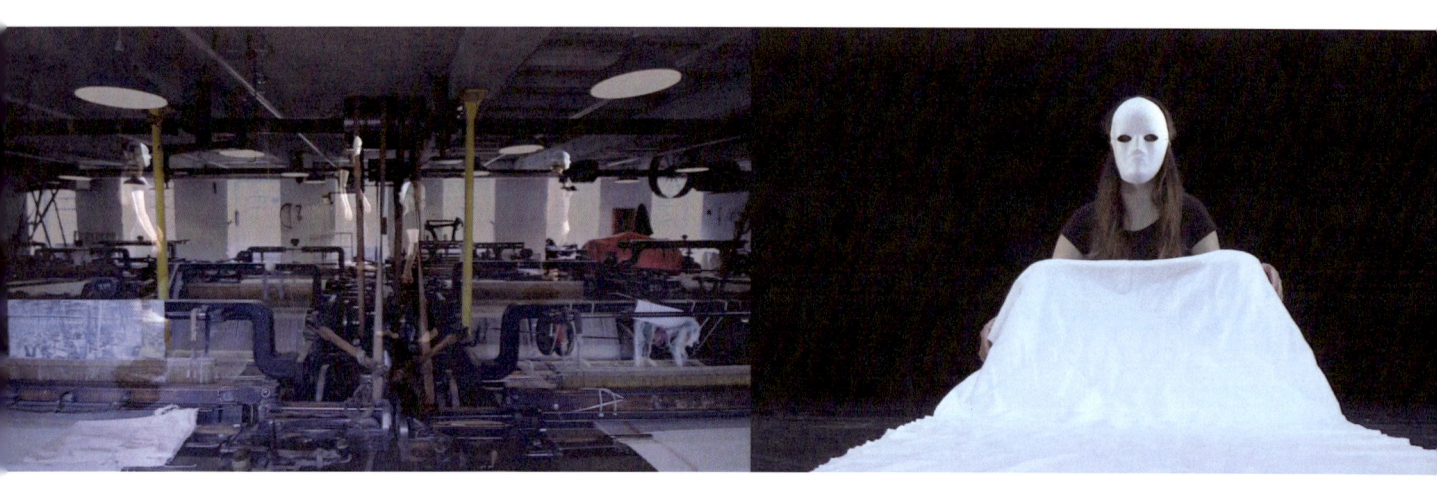

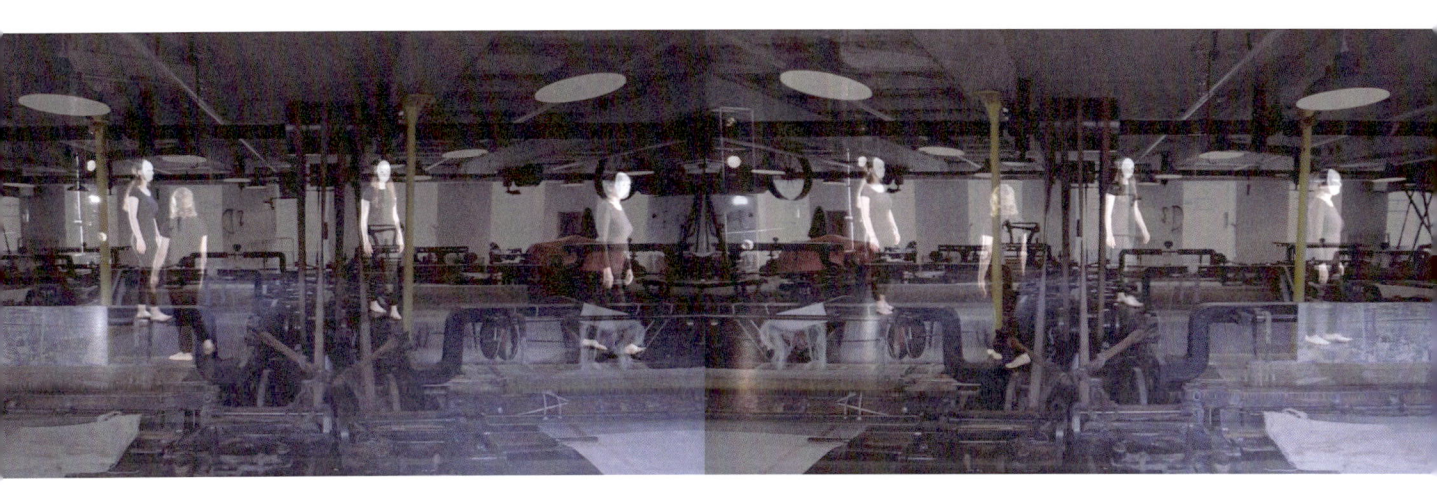

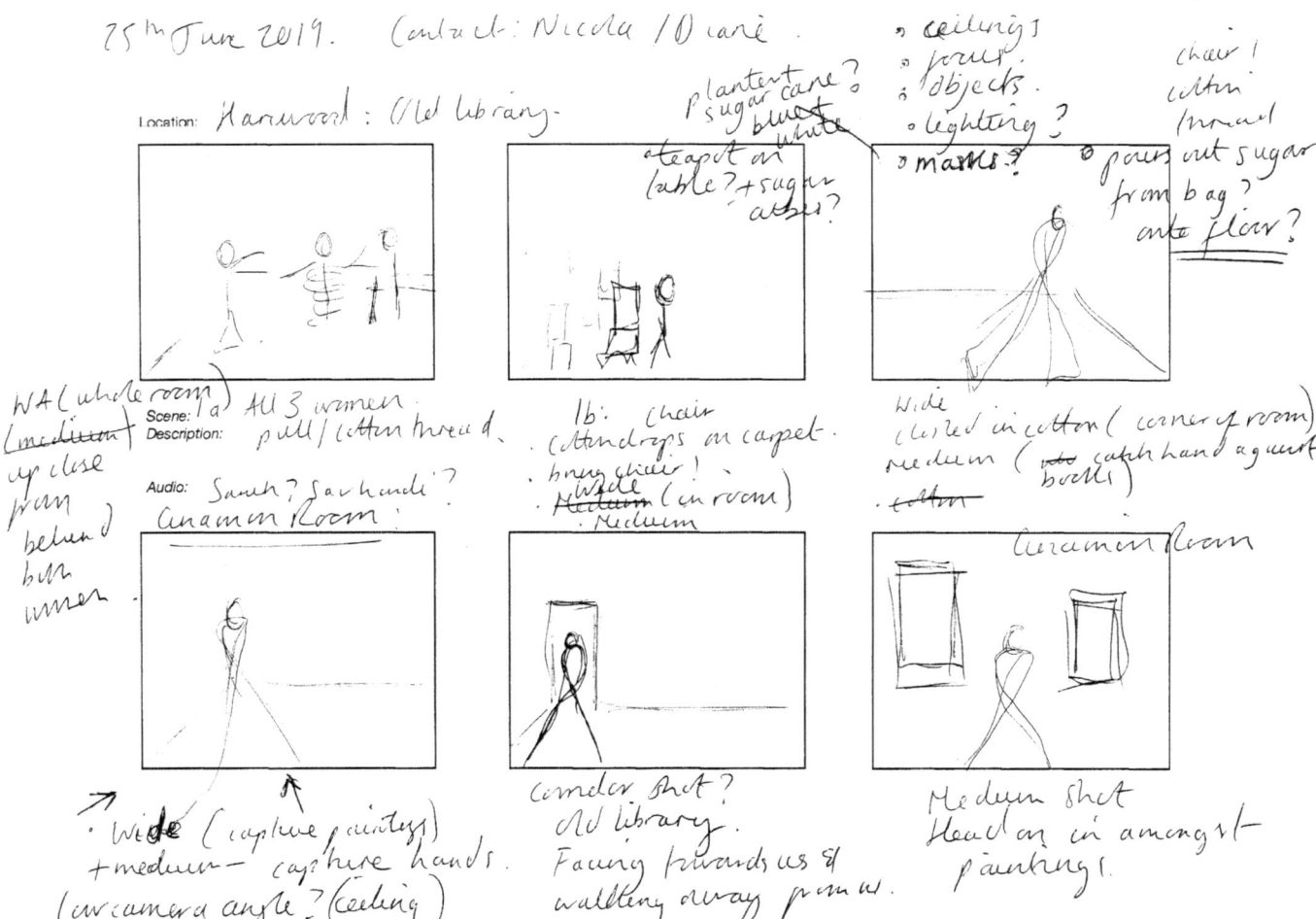

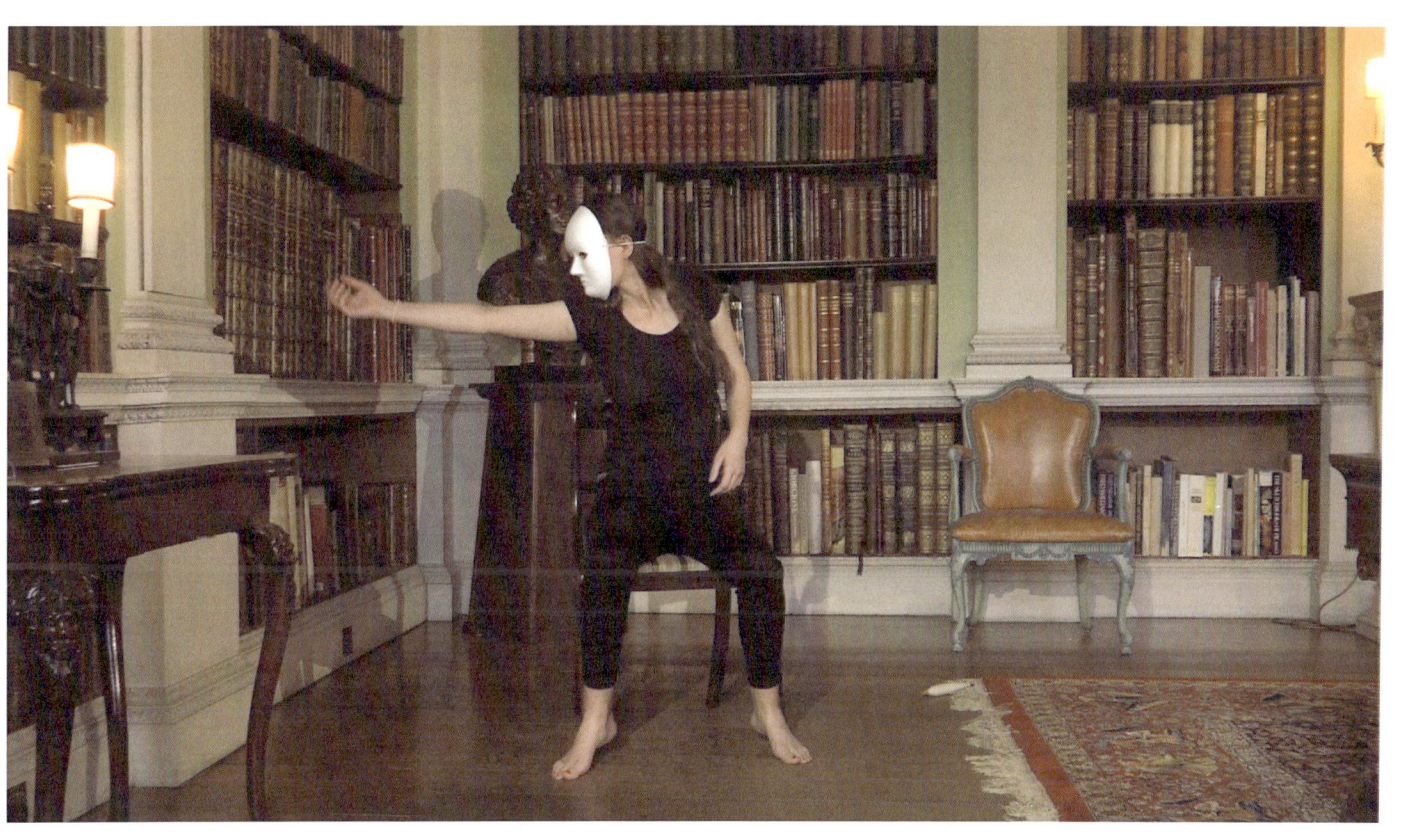

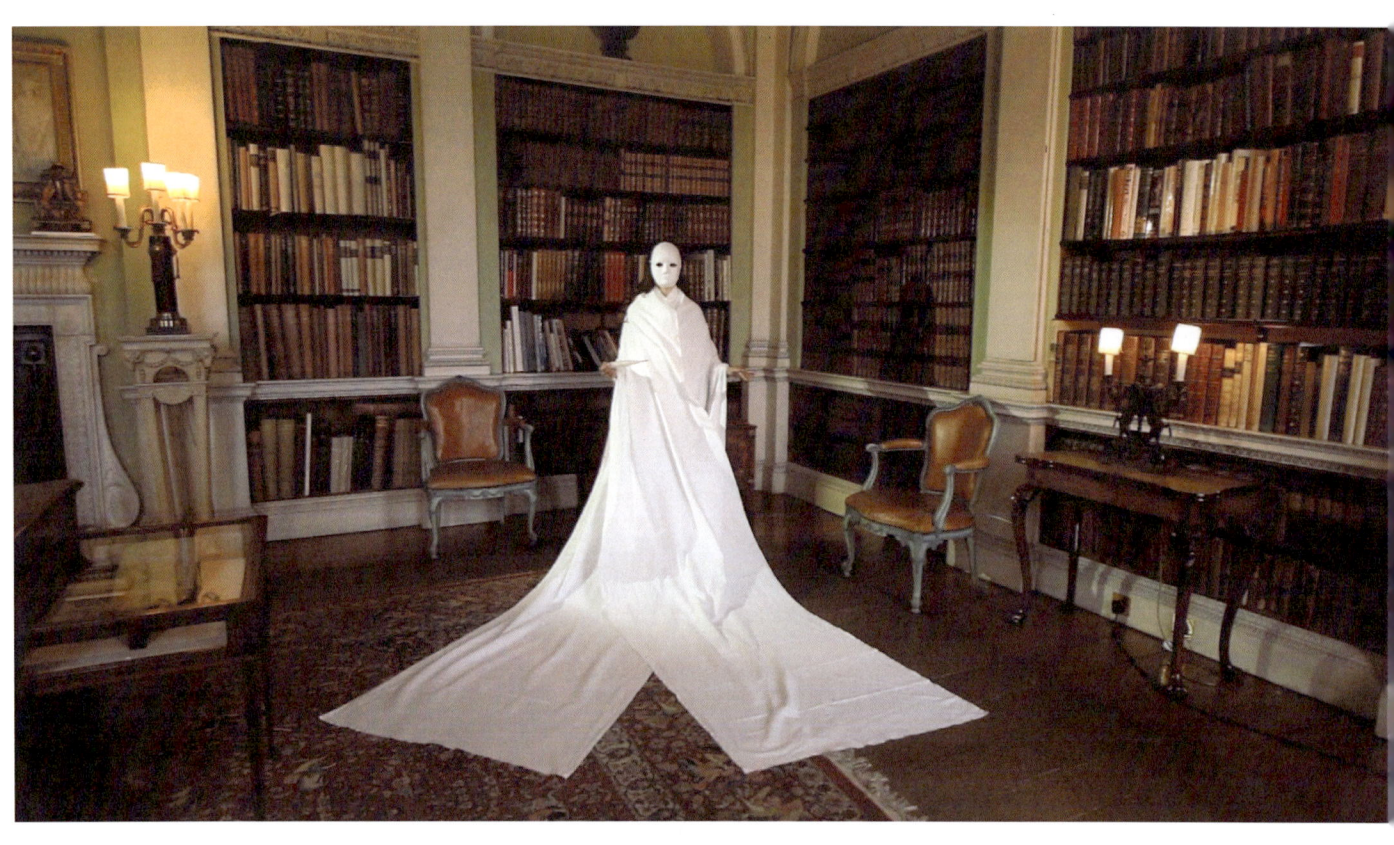

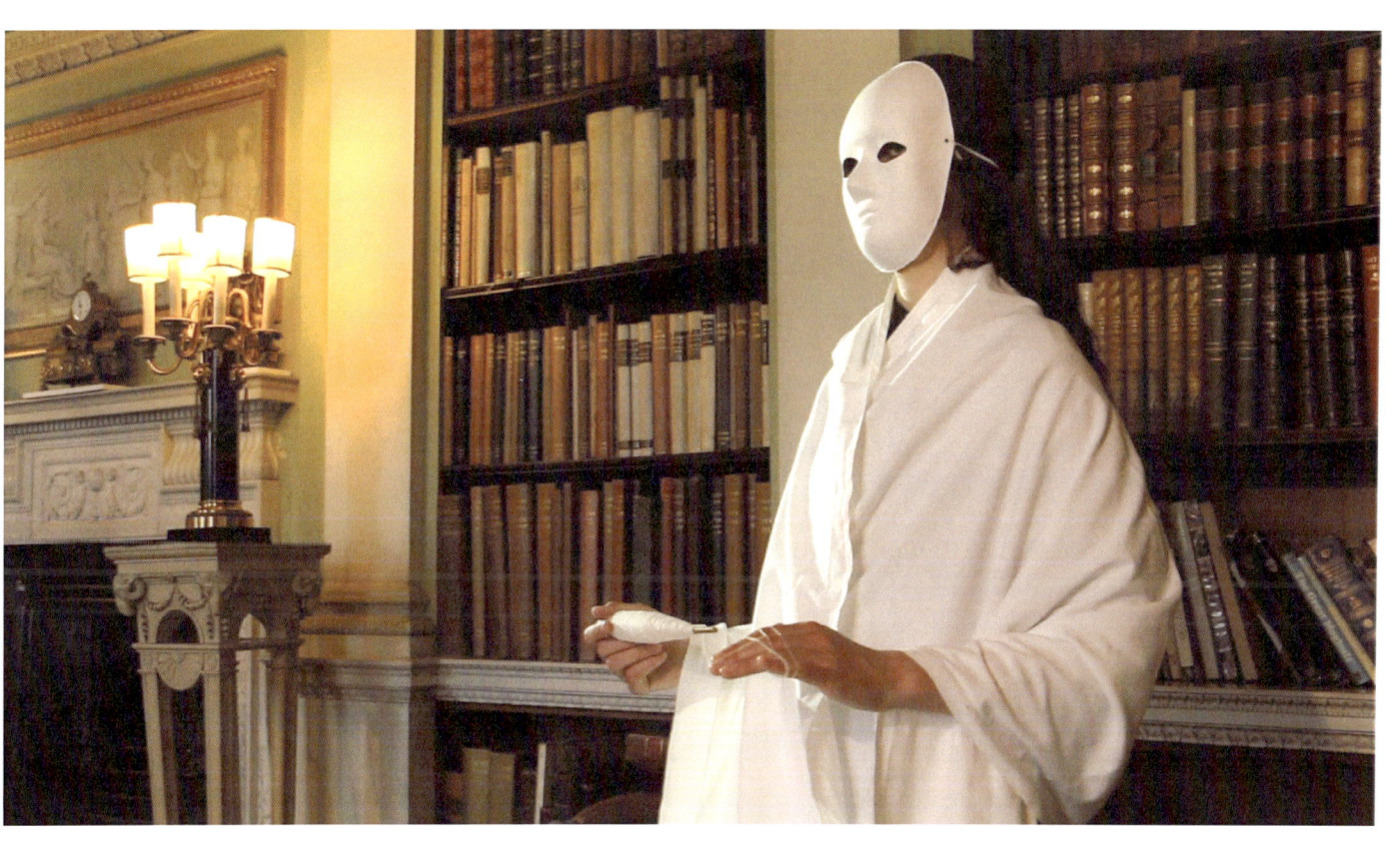

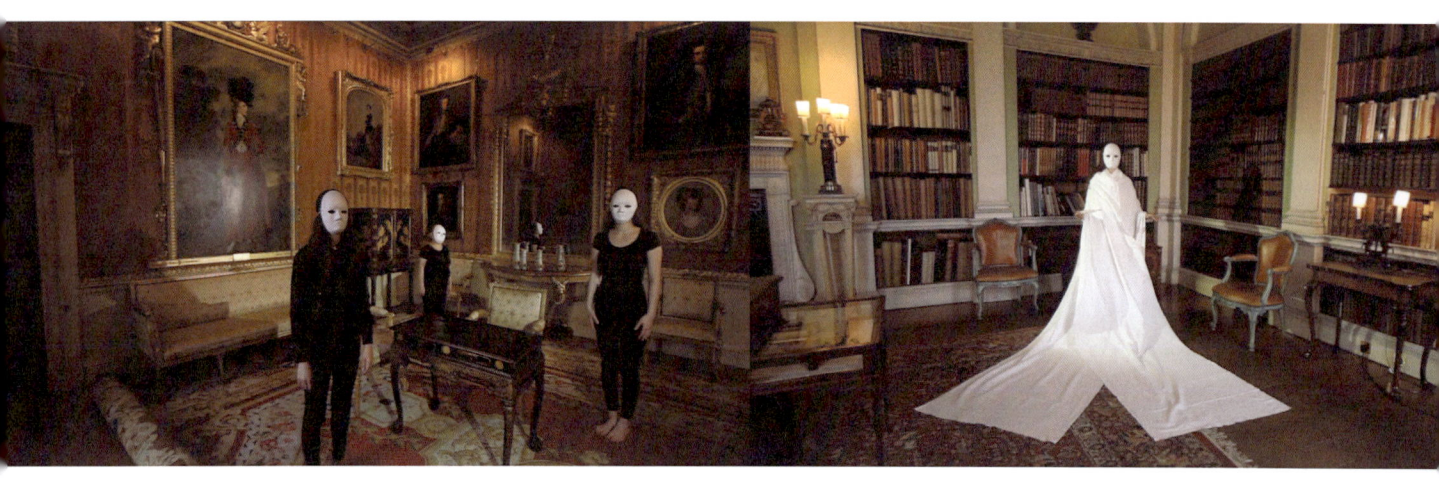

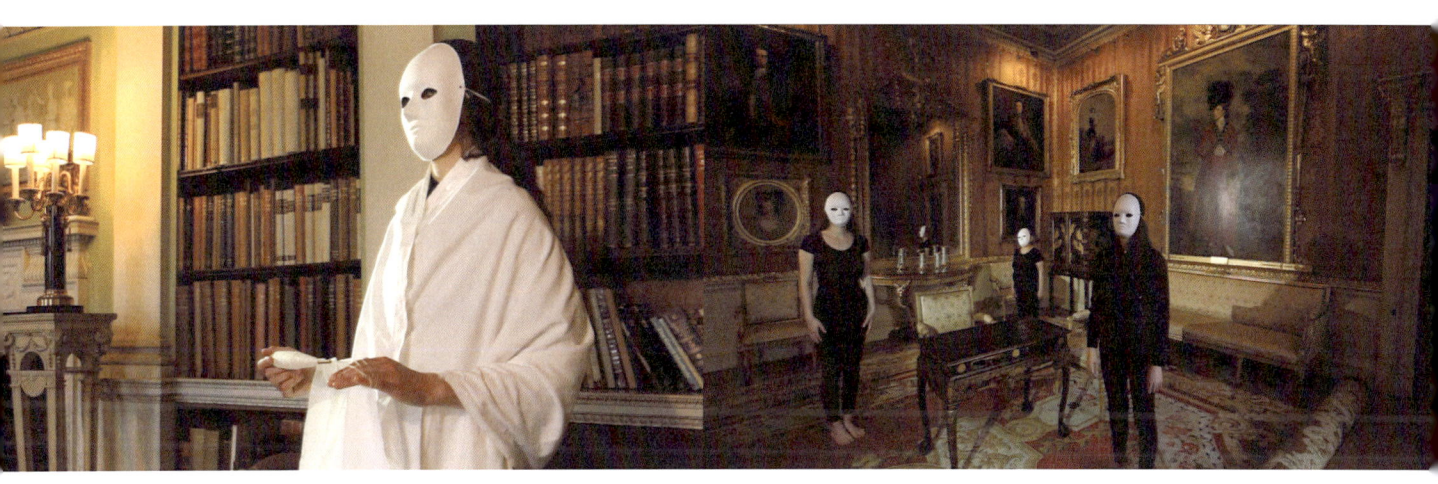

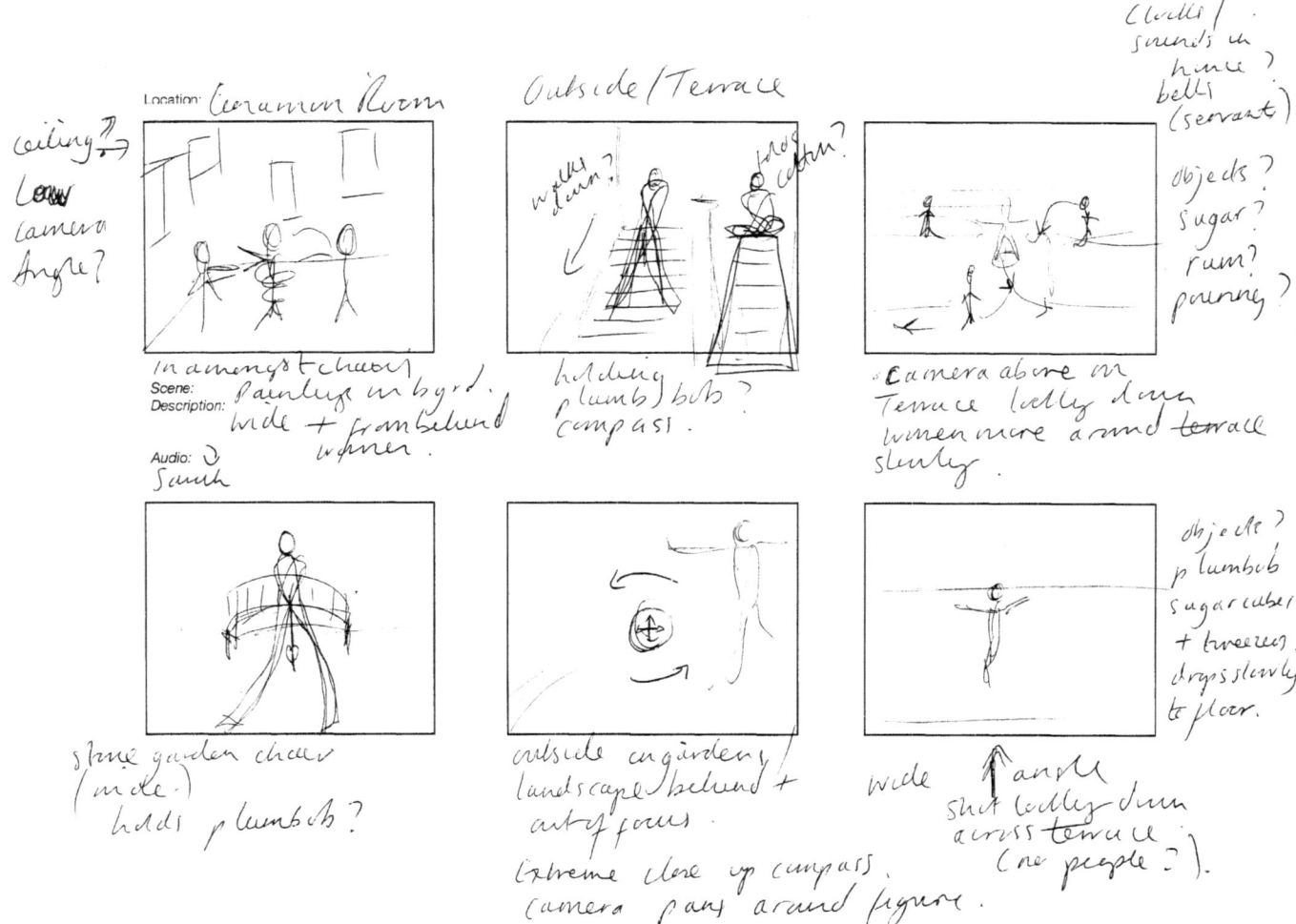

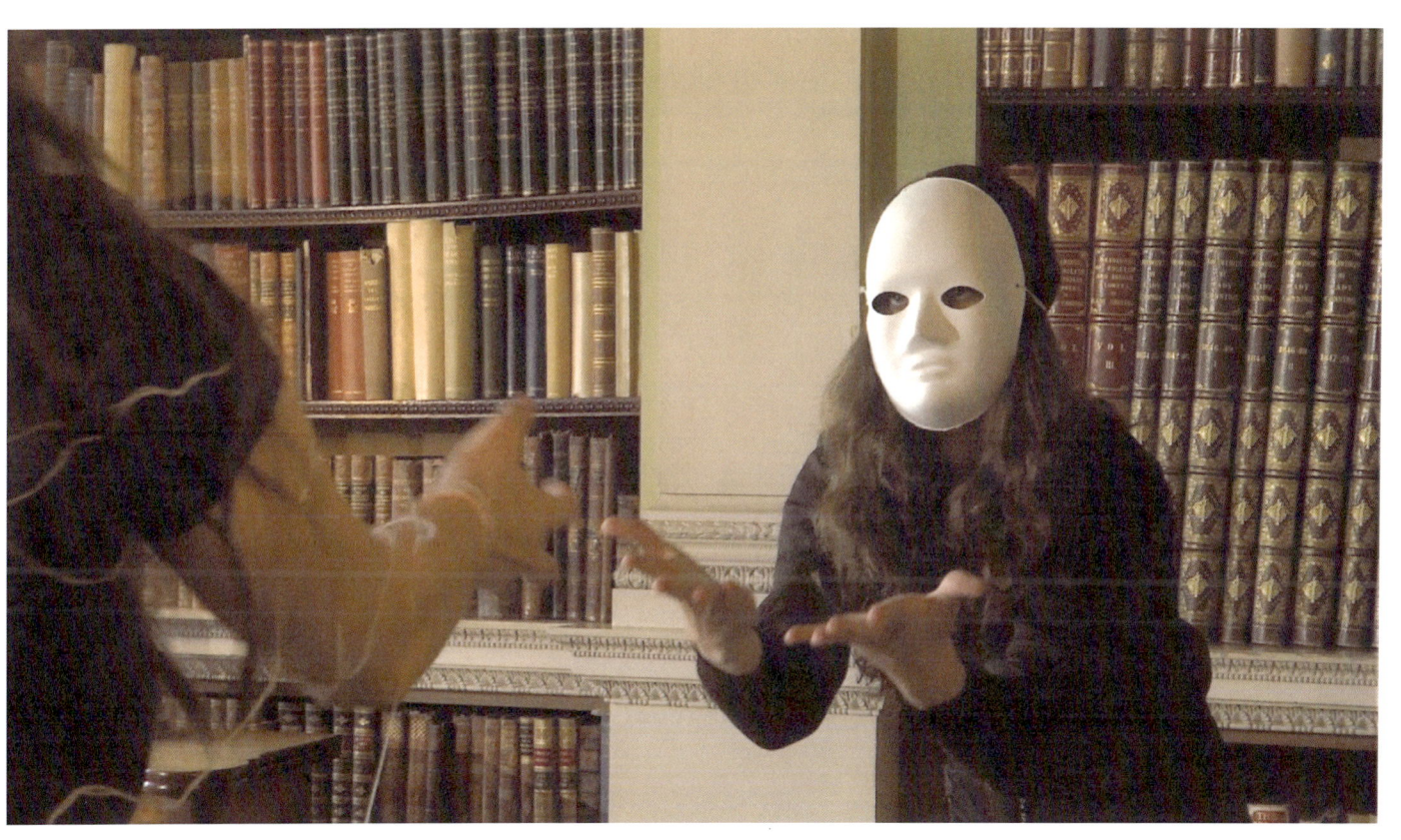

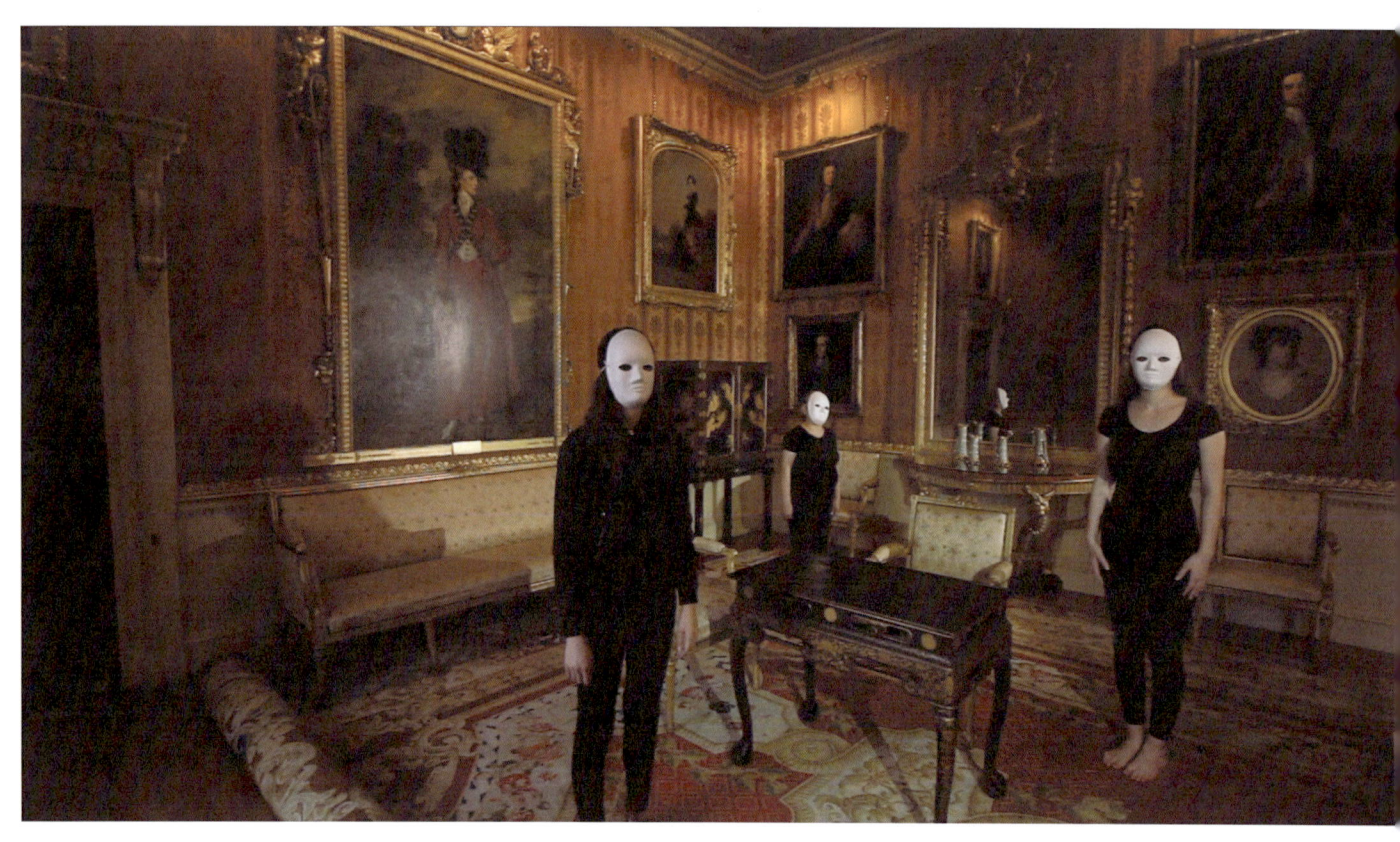

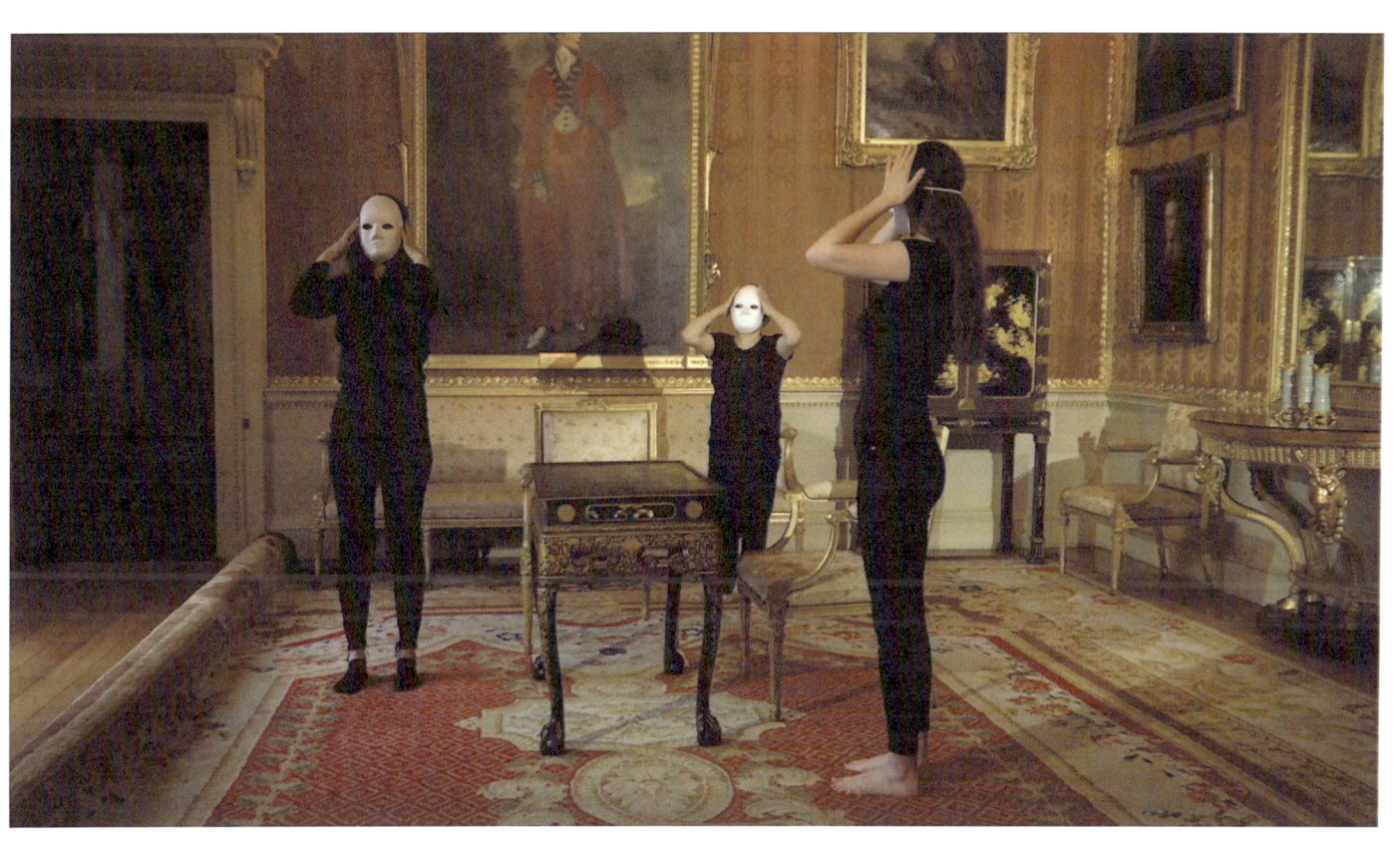

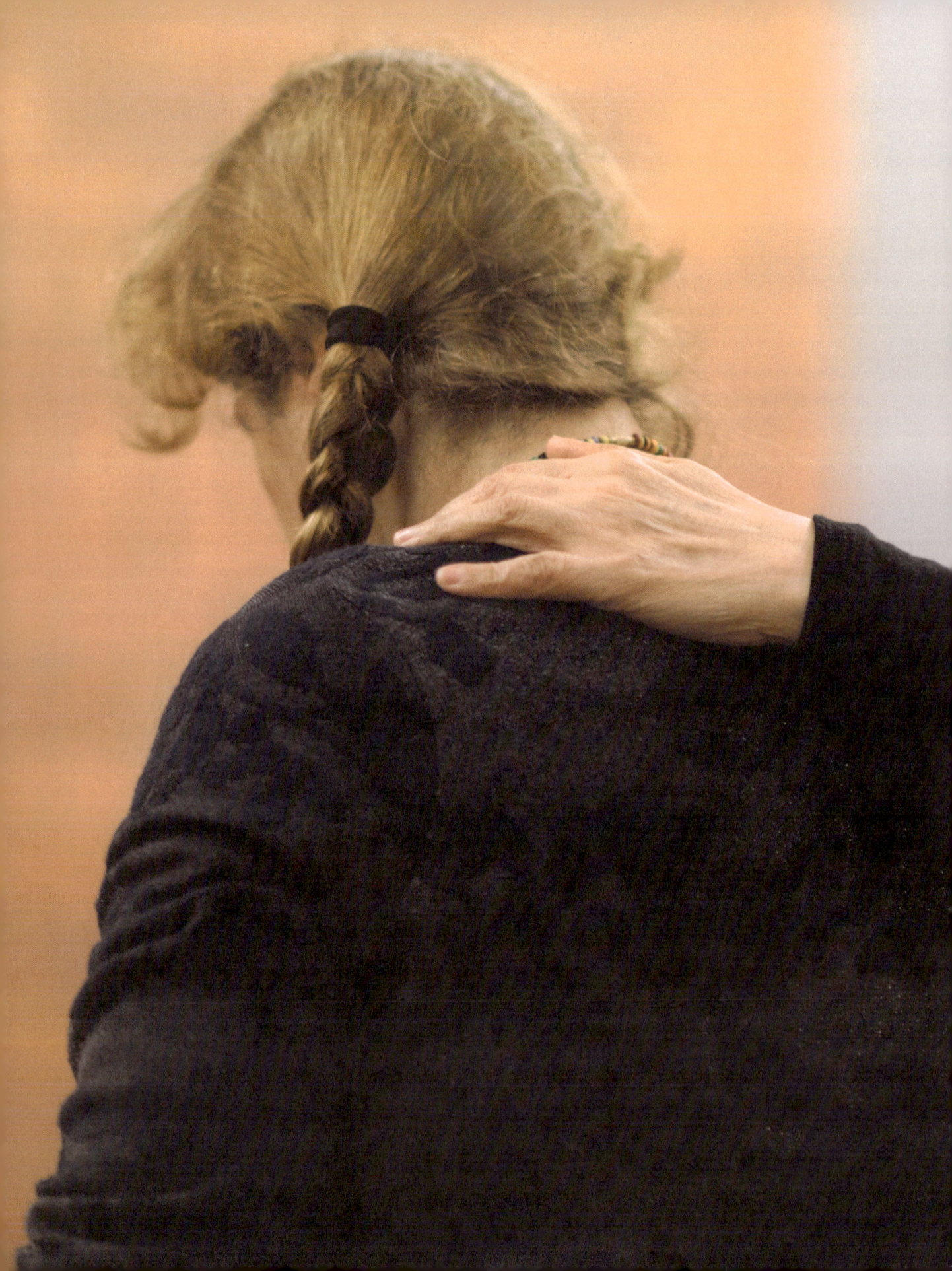

Conversations with the women

Week 2: OPPRESSOR/ OPPRESSED

Magdalen: "FALL So you have to find a way to fall, what does fall mean to you? Does fall always mean to go to the ground? You also have RISE, what does rise make you think of?"

Judith: "Rise up."

Magdalen: "Coming up from somewhere. What about REACH?" [woman enacts movement] What about curl? When you curl up."

Judith: "Feelings."

Magdalen: "Yes so what kind of feelings can make us curl up in a ball. Or you know when you have an ice cream and you put the spoon on it, and as you're running the spoon it curls, or your hair it curls, how can we show that in movement?

"We're going to look at two words, to be oppressed or suppressed, and to be the oppressor. Does anyone understand what oppressor means? So, if you bully… or if someones a dictator and they say 'you do it my way! You do it my way!' That's oppressing someone, so you're not free, you're freedom in someway is"—

Becky: "It's like someone is trying to push you to do something you're not expecting to do."

Magdalen: "Yes! That's oppressing someone because you haven't got that freedom to have your say. So in this piece we're going to look at the words and the movements we already have. We're going to look at oppressed and oppressor. And oppressor is the person who's telling you 'you have no rights I'm telling you what to do' and to be oppressed is the victim, the person who's being pushed, controlled, and the other person is going to push you, block you —"

Becky: "It's like you're in the middle of the group, you try yourself to go out but you can't, some other people they are pushing you, like when we're playing something… some other people want you to join their group and you refuse it. They will push you there in order to do it."

Magdalen: "So gangs and things like this is very oppressive.

"So I'm oppressing her, just from pushing her down, and turning her around, and moving her away [demonstrates this in movement] So how does it feel when I'm doing that to you?

"Another way of oppressing, is if someone just comes over you, or if they cover you, you don't want to be covered, you want to be free."

Becky: "It's like if I'm trying to go forward and you push me back."

Magdalen: "But in movement we can't be very aggressive, we can't kick or punch so we have to do it in a different way, so we do it by folding over or by manipulating how they move, eg. 'You can't have that, go over there!' [demonstrates]. So it's taking away that right.

"So what you're going to do in the next thing, is looking at these movements and also putting in movements of your own, you're going to look in the relationship of the dance. You've got a full set of movements here and a full set of movements there and you're going to change that meaning, looking at who will be oppressing [Diana demonstrates her movements, Magdalen acts as the oppressor and makes changes to her movements] So I'm making her do that movement rather than her choosing to do that movement. So your partner will have to instigate those movements, of where the modes of control will be, it might change your movement. So the oppressor can instigate those movements, so you're actually controlling what she does, rather than her doing it herself."

Week 3: STILLNESS, FALL, RISE, REACH, CURL

Magdalen: "So what I want you to do in your three, is to look at these words and come up with a narrative. So you can start maybe each of you coming up with a movement for these five words individually… STILLNESS, FALL, RISE, REACH, CURL.

"So this one will be an independent task, so you will think of still, fall, rise, reach, curl, but it has to be different.

"A different way of still… still could be lying down, it could be standing, it could be crouched over, it's your moment of stillness and you have to hold that moment of stillness for maybe 8 counts. And then different ways of falling, but it has to be different, it can't be the same way.

"And then rise, there's different ways of rising… you could already be standing and then just stretch your arms.

"And then reach, three different ways of reaching (one each).

"And then different ways of curling, it could be curl, or curling the cotton around if you want to start using something like this [Magdalen curls the cotton thread around her fingers] snap, pull, drop…. It's up to you, but it's an individual bit. So this is a moment just for you, to come up with those five words, these movements will be used in the piece."

Week 4: HOLD, TURN, TRAVEL, BLOCK, PUSH

Magdalen: "How can someone oppress you as a grown up, what can they say to you to oppress you? Example? So lets say you want to go somewhere"—

Isabella: "Go there!" [gives orders]

Magdalen: "Yes they order you, they tell you where to go, how to dress… And if the person don't want to do it, what can that person do to make you do it? What can some people do to make you do something you don't want to do?"

Isabella: "Like when your family makes you go."

Diana: "They press you."

Magdalen: "But how?"

Diana: "I'm going to kill you!" [jokingly]

Magdalen: "So threaten."

Isabella: "Can we practice?!" [jokingly]

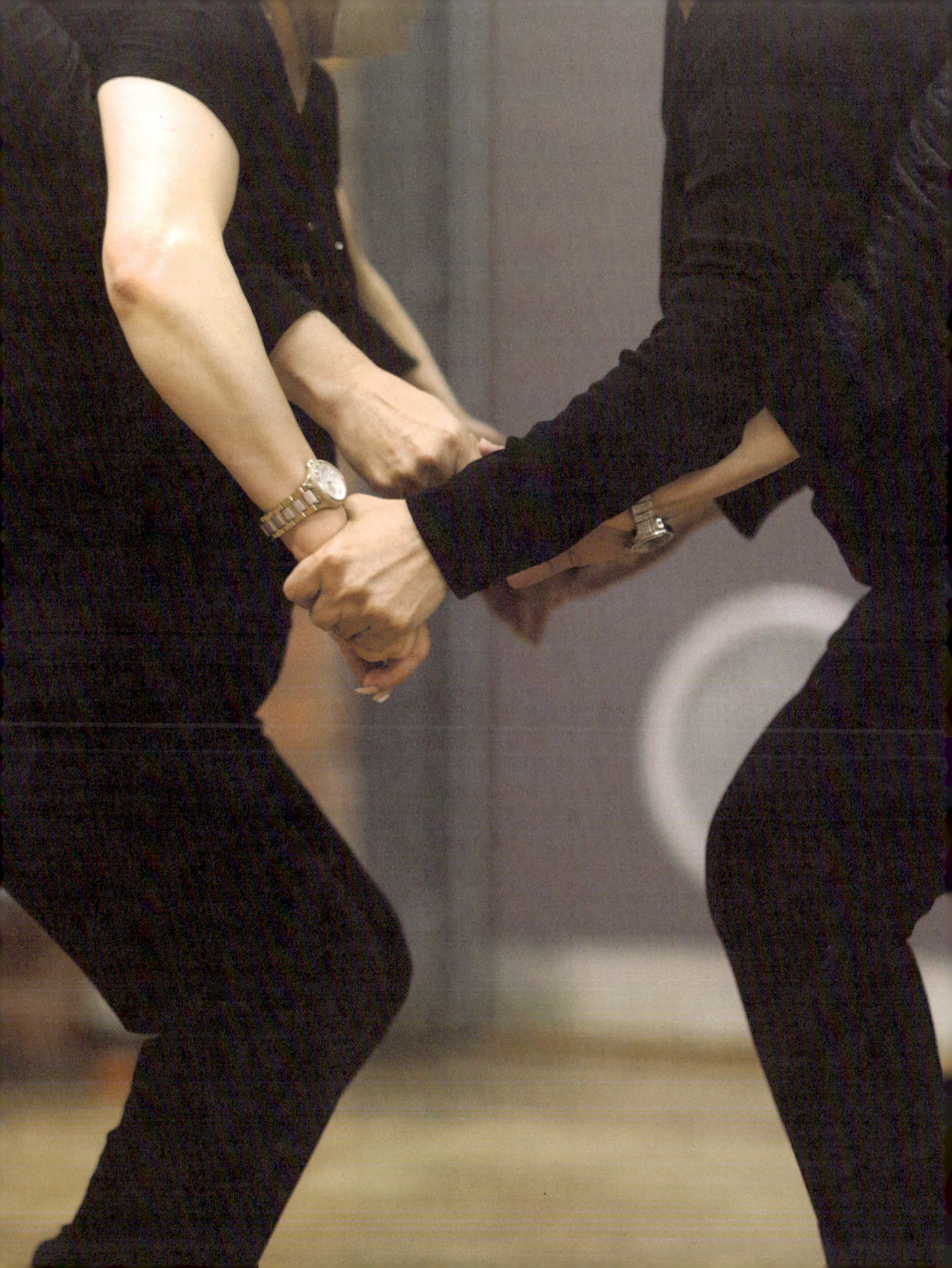

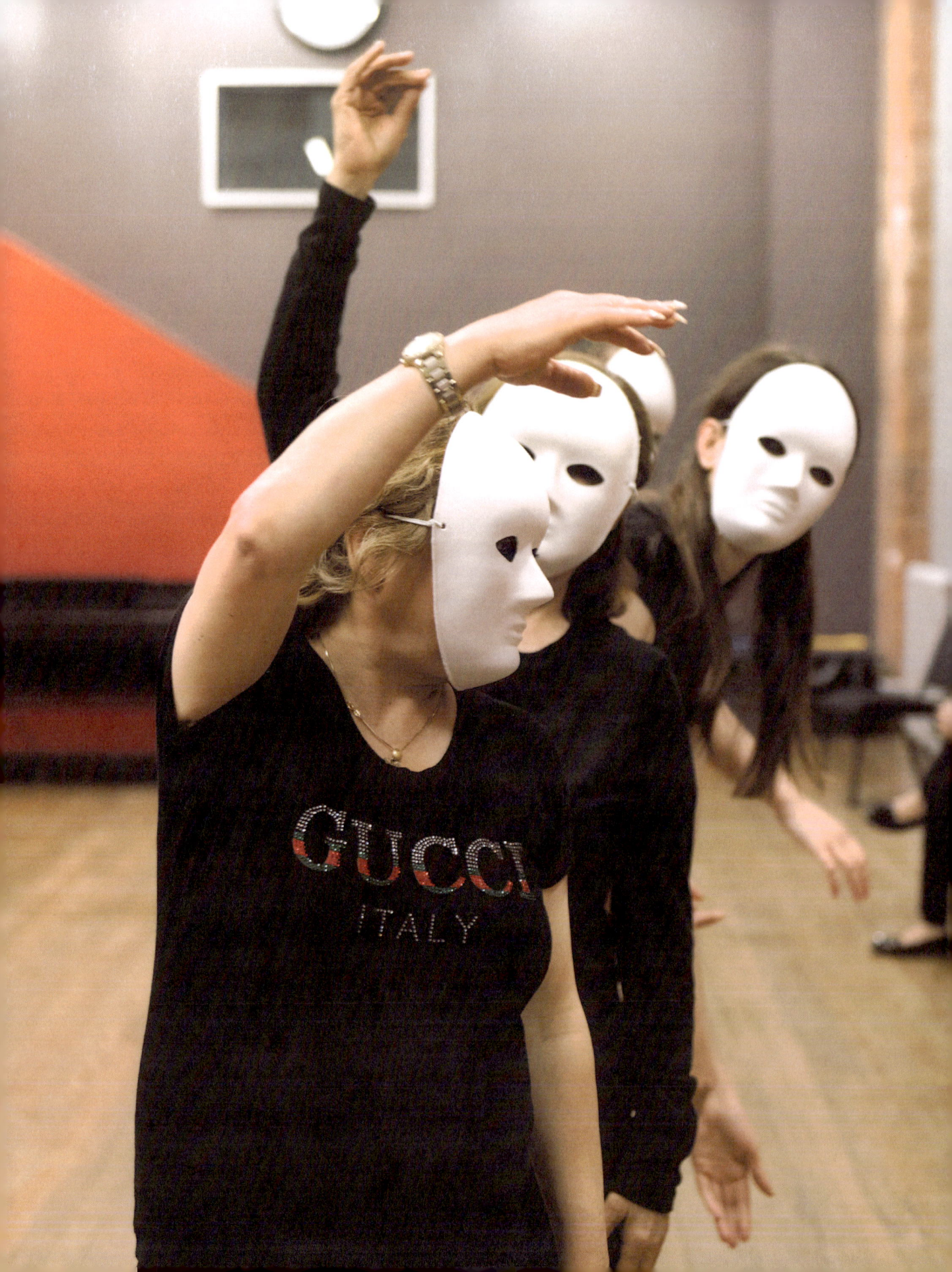

Magdalen: "No don't beat her up! [laughs]

"So when you're doing these movements, you're threatening and ordering. It's much more harsh.

"Do you think people who oppress people think about others feelings?"

Diana: "No."

Isabella: "No."

Magdalen: "No because if they did they wouldn't do it. Do you think they enjoy?"

Diana: "If they do it, should be happy."

Magdalen: "So when we're do this one we're going to look at maximum control, so you know when you said, 'take that!' 'go there!' Do you think they know what they're doing?"

Isabella: "Yeah."

Magdalen: "Do you think they have a plan in their head or they're just random?"

Diana: "No plan, I don't think."

Magdalen: "HOLD, so how would you hold someone in an oppressive way? Can you demonstrate one of you holding someone in an oppressive way?

"When you are being oppressed, do you want to stand there and take it, or go?"

Isabella: "To go."

Magdalen: "So one of you will have to decide who that bully will be."

Isabella: "I don't want to be oppressed."

Magdalen: "Why don't you want to do that one? You don't feel comfortable?"

Isabella: "No."

Magdalen: "No, she doesn't have to. So let's do Hold, Turn, Travel, Block, Push... and we won't put names to it."

Magdalen Bartlett Luambia is a freelance producer and choreographer based in Manchester.

* All names have been changed to protect the identity of the women.

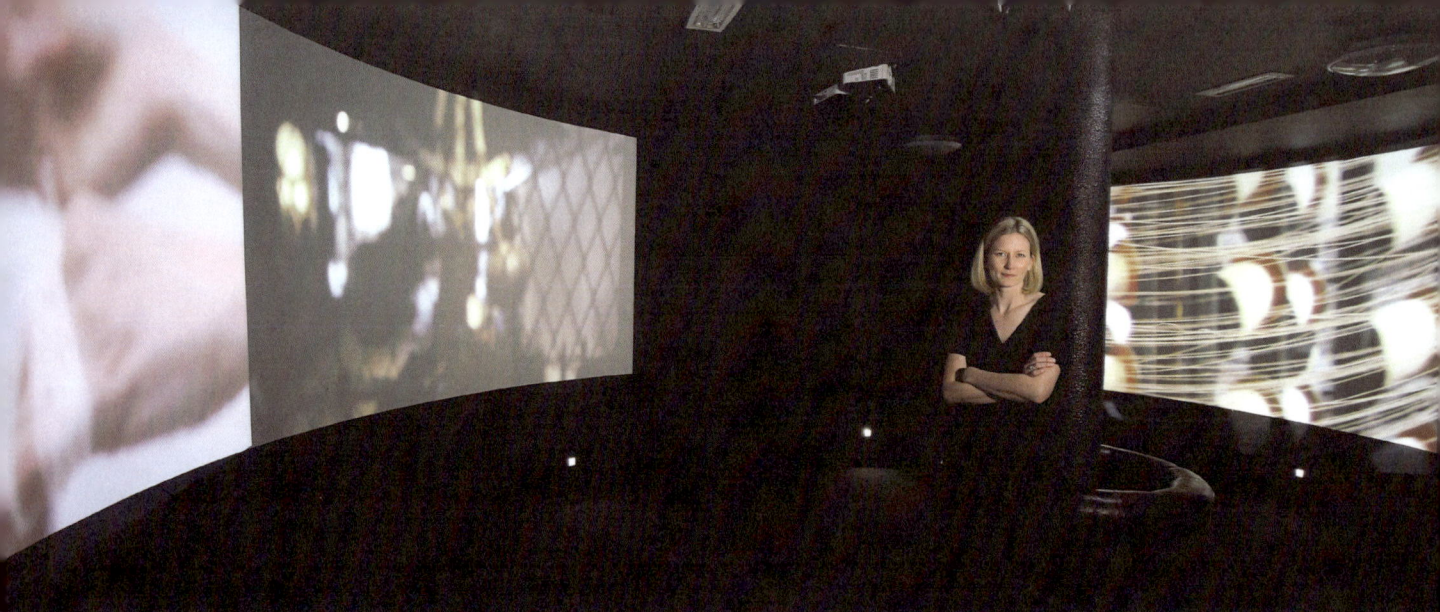

Biography

b. 1983

EDUCATION

MA Fine Art, 1st Class Honours with distinction. Edinburgh University/ Edinburgh College of Art 2001- 2006.

SELECTED EXHIBITIONS

2019 Am I not a woman and a sister, The International Slavery Museum, Liverpool

2019 Time After [ ] After Time, The Briggait Wasps Studios Glasgow

2019 Habeas Corpus, Manchester Cathedral

2019 Print: A Cataylst for Social Change, Bury Art Museum

2019 Displaced, The Travelling Gallery, Scotland (touring)

2018 In- Transit, Canada House Manchester

2018 Radical and Real Film Shorts, HOME Manchester

2017 Mediterranea, DOK Artist Space, Edinburgh

2017 Mediterranea, Nomas Projects, Dundee

2017 In- Transit, Genesis Centre, Paris

2017 IWAYA Community Arts Festival, Lagos Nigeria

2017 In Nothing Flat, Studiobook 17, Manchester

2017 Greater Manchester Art Prize

2017 Framing the Crisis, System Gallery, Newcastle

2016 Europa, Transition Gallery, London

2013 Tracing Presence, The People's History Museum in conjunction with Manchester University and Platforma Festival.

2012 Tracing Presence, The Mustard Tree, in partnership with The Boaz Trust Manchester.

RESIDENCIES

2019 The International Slavery Museum Archives & Library, Liverpool

2017, 2018 The Castlefield Gallery New Art Spaces, Manchester

2011 -2012 The Mustard Tree / The Boaz Trust, Manchester

SELECTED PUBLICATIONS/ PRESS

BBC Africa 'What's New?' (Episode 74) 2nd December 2019.

'Slavery museum in Liverpool aims to confront painful legacy' by Russell Contreras, The Associated Press. Article published in The New York Times December 18th 2019

BBC Radio Merseyside, Interview with Ngunan Adamu and Curator Jean Francois Manicom, Sunday 15th December 2019

'Taking a look at modern slavery: exhibition at city's dockside museum provides welcome voice for contemporary victims' by Lorna Hughes, Liverpool Echo Tuesday 31st December 2019

ITV Granada News, Friday 15th November 2019

'Modern day slavery put in spotlight' John Moores Journalism, 20th November 2019, by Lewis Batty

'A Belonging Project' by Jonathan Evans, Artlyst 7th Sept 2019

AWARDS

2019 National Lottery Project Grant, Arts Council England

2017 Selected for Studiobook 17 Artist Professional Development Programme produced by Mark Devereux Projects

2015, 2017 Seedbed Grant

2006 The Andrew Grant Bequest, Edinburgh College of Art

Am I not a woman and a sister has been supported using public funding by the National Lottery through Arts Council England.

With special thanks to The International Slavery Museum & National Museums Liverpool, City Hearts and Harewood House Trust.

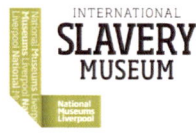 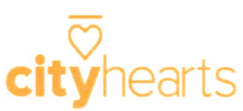 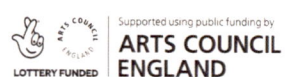 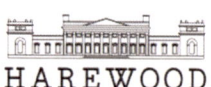

www.ingramcontent.com/pod-product-compliance
Lightning Source LLC
Chambersburg PA
CBRC100912220526
45473CB00011B/2870